THE MAKING OF WAKEFIELD

Wood Street in the 1880s.
Yorkshire Archaeological Society

THE MAKING OF
WAKEFIELD
1801–1900

KATE TAYLOR

Series Editor
Brian Elliott

Wharncliffe Books

First published in Great Britain in 2008 by
Wharncliffe Books
an imprint of
Pen and Sword Books Limited,
47 Church Street, Barnsley,
South Yorkshire. S70 2AS

ISBN: 978 1 845630 78 2

A CIP catalogue record of this book is available from the
British Library.

Typeset in 10/12pt Plantin by
Pen and Sword Books Ltd

Printed in the United Kingdom by
CPI UK

Pen & Sword Books Ltd incorporates the imprints of
Pen & Sword Aviation, Pen & Sword Maritime,
Pen & Sword Military, Wharncliffe Local History, Pen & Sword Select,
Pen & Sword Military Classics, Leo Cooper, Remember When, Seaforth Publishing
and Frontline Publishing

For a complete list of Pen & Sword titles please contact:
PEN & SWORD BOOKS LIMITED
47 Church Street, Barnsley, South Yorkshire, S70 2AS, England.
E-mail: enquiries@pen-and-sword.co.uk
Website: www.pen-and-sword.co.uk

Contents

Introduction 7

Chapter 1 **Administration and Politics**
    The Street Commissioners 11
    Policing and keeping order 14
    The Board of Guardians 23
    Wakefield becomes a Municipal Borough 25
    The diminution of Manorial powers 33
    Representation in Parliament 36
    Wakefield becomes the seat of the West Riding
        County Council 41

Chapter 2 **Amenities**
    Provision for the sick and poor 43
    The Borough Cemetery 56
    The water supply 57
    Lighting 60
    The Post Office 62
    Local Newspapers 64
    The Fire Service 67

Chapter 3 **Communication, Trade and Industry**
    The waterways 70
    The roads 73
    The railways 74
    The banks 76
    Coalmining 80
    Textiles 82
    The markets 86
    Some other industries and enterprises 91

Chapter 4 **Religion – Growth, Concern and Conflict**
    Nonconformity and its varied forms 98
    The Anglican churches 103
    Catholicism – Roman and Anglican 111
    Missionary activities 113
    Resisting the church rate 115

The renewal of places of worship......................116
A major anniversary 117
Wakefield hosts the national Church Congress.........117
Wakefield becomes a Diocese 118

Chapter 5 **Education**
Schools administered by the Governors of the
    Wakefield Charities 122
Sunday Schools 126
The first elementary schools.........................127
The development of the Church of England
    (National) schools 129
Nonconformist and non-sectarian schools 131
A Roman Catholic elementary school...................134
Infant education and Samuel Wilderspin 135
The Ragged Schools 137
Private Schools......................................138
The School Board 139
Adult Education 142

Chapter 6 **Leisure and Entertainment**
Theatres and Music Halls.............................147
Balls and bazaars....................................155
Circuses and other visiting shows 158
Excursions...160
Open space...161
Clubs and Societies..................................165
Wakefield regattas and races.........................168
Public Baths...170
Wakefield en fete....................................171

Bibliography...172

Index..174

$\mathcal{I}$NTRODUCTION

Wakefield was already a prosperous market town in the fourteenth century when its inhabitants rebuilt the parish church (now Wakefield Cathedral) and provided a handsome stone bridge, replacing a wooden one, across the Calder. In subsequent centuries it continued to develop. Keith Cowland, in a study of the urban growth of Wakefield 1801-1901, noted that 'Towards the end of the eighteenth century [it] enjoyed a high esteem as the county administrative centre for the West Riding, as a manufacturing town for wool and worsted and as a merchanting centre for wool, corn and coal. Its industrial structure was dominated by the woollen and worsted manufacturers and merchants, the dyers, the scribbling millers and the corn traders.'

Wakefield was described in 1812 as one of the handsomest and most populous towns in the West Riding. The writer went on: 'Most of the streets are regular, handsome and spacious and many of the houses, which are generally constructed of brick, are large, lofty and elegant.' Wakefield's higher-class residents lived in the new developments of St John's and South Parade and in the developing areas of Bond Street, Westfield Road, St John's Grove (now College Grove Road) and in Southgate, New Wells and Thornhill Street.

So what was distinctive about the nineteenth century? For the most part, developments in Wakefield reflected national trends: there was an increasingly democratic local-government system with its increasing involvement in the provision of what had earlier been the province of churches and chapels or commercial companies – schools, a cemetery, and swimming baths, for example. Wakefield reflected the national developments, too, in the provision of utilities – gas, water and an electricity supply. Setting aside a possible medieval hospital which possibly housed lepers, it got its first hospitals in the nineteenth century. It saw the development of mass production in mills and factories. It saw the origins of an educational system for the masses, based not on acquiring Latin, Greek and some philosophy, but on learning mathematics and spelling, historical and geographical facts, by rote, with monitors passing on mechanically the lessons handed out to them by teachers.

As elsewhere, its administration and business affairs were male-dominated. Anglican clergy and Nonconformist ministers were significant figures in public affairs well beyond those of church and chapel, appearing on numerous public platforms. Local 'gentry' still mattered (some of them, like the baronet Edward Green, climbing the social staircase through industry) although the role of the gentry diminished in the course of the century as leading industrialists began to take their place on public platforms or as patrons of social events.

But women played a leading role in charitable work, running, for example, soup kitchens and other welfare services. Women who qualified as ratepayers were able to vote for members of the Board of Guardians from its inception, of the town council from 1869, and for members of Wakefield's first School Board in 1871. The first Wakefield women actually to sit on an elected administrative body were those appointed to the Board of Guardians for the period 1895-8.

Politically, Wakefield was fairly evenly divided between the Tories and the Whigs/Liberals/Radicals. Labour made some little incursion in the 1890s with the election of Independent Labour members to the Council and to the School Board.

What was particular about Wakefield in our period? For centuries the county town of the West Riding, it became at the end of the century the administrative headquarters of the great West Riding County Council. It also became the centre of a new Anglican diocese with its parish church elevated to the status of a cathedral. As a consequence it also became, in 1888, a city. Much of the topography of the town centre today is a legacy of the nineteenth century, including a number of new streets and the splendid run of public buildings that dominate Wood Street.

Primarily this book is about the area that became the municipal borough in 1848 but the ecclesiastical parish of Wakefield was much larger, embracing the townships of Stanley cum Wrenthorpe and of Alverthorpe with Thornes, and frequent reference is made to these and to the adjacent township of Sandal.

This book lacks the scope to say much about the very many individual men (and women) who made Wakefield what it was in the nineteenth century. As examples, mention might be made here of Samuel Sharp (1773-1855), vicar of Wakefield from 1810 until his death, who took an active part in many local enterprises and who masterminded the renewal of the bridge chantry, and of the radical George William Harrison (1806-1860), who was a cornfactor, campaigner against what he saw as impositions (the church rate and the requirements of the soke), and supporter of the coalminers during the 1844 strike, who became Wakefield's first mayor. Then there was Henry Lee (1821-1893), industrialist, Liberal town councillor for more than thirty years, three times Mayor of Wakefield, a promoter of the Model Lodging House, and the prime mover in the local authority's measures to provide a supply of excellent water, who was made the first Freeman of the newly created city in 1888. And there was the Tory Edward Green (1831-1923), again an industrialist (second generation), the first chairman of Wakefield School Board, and member of Parliament for Wakefield from 1880-1892.

Anyone who seeks to write about the history of Wakefield must be indebted to J W Walker and his pioneer book, *Wakefield, its History and its People*. Walker amassed a most useful collection of photographs of Wakefield, primarily of the 1880s, and these are now held by the Yorkshire Archaeological Society. A good many appear in this book. But the present writer has made considerably more use of the more recent work of the leading Wakefield and regional historian, John Goodchild and is indebted to him for very considerable information and advice and for the opportunity to use the resources of his local history study centre.

Much of the material for this book has been derived from a lengthy study of Wakefield newspapers, held at the Local Studies department of Wakefield MDC Library Service. Other material has come from the manuscript volumes of Street Commissioners' Minutes, Council Minutes and the West Riding Quarter Sessions Order Books kept by the West Yorkshire Archive Service at the Registry of Deeds in Wakefield. I am grateful to the staff of both bodies for their untiring and friendly assistance. Thanks are due, too, to Commissioning Editor, Brian Elliott, at Wharncliffe Books and to his colleagues in design, production and marketing.

1   *A*DMINISTRATION AND POLITICS

At the beginning of the nineteenth century administration in Wakefield lay in the hands of a range of bodies. It was (with the exception of the small areas of the Rectory Manor of Wakefield or belonging to the Manor of Newland) a part of the great Manor of Wakefield under whose jurisdiction the Constables and Pindars were appointed, weights and measures were tested, small debts were claimed, fairs and markets were held, and copyhold property was transferred. The Manorial soke rights had been separated from the Manor itself in the reign of James I, but Wakefield people were still required to take their corn, grain and malt to be ground at the soke mill and could legitimately buy flour only that had been milled there. Since 1771 the paving, cleansing and sewering of the main streets had been in the hands of a body of Street Commissioners, established under an Act of Parliament, who met in the chamber above the Market Cross (Figure 1). A further act of 1796 allowed them to light the streets and to employ watchmen at night. Policing during the day was the responsibility of the Constable and his deputies. The overall administrative body was the magistracy. Justices of the peace, nominated by the Lord Lieutenant, held a wide range of responsibilities beyond maintaining law and order.

Figure 1: The Market Cross. *Yorkshire Archaeological Society*

Among other things they provided the Registry of Deeds for properties not held by copyhold, they registered Nonconformist places of worship and Friendly Societies, they licensed inns, alehouses, troupes of travelling actors, and private lunatic asylums, they reimbursed the county's coroners, and, via their Clerk of the

Figure 2: The Probate Office. *The author*

Peace, issued game certificates. The magistrates were also the body responsible for maintaining Wakefield's bridges and for the formal appointment of the Overseers of the Poor, and the Surveyors of Highways for Wakefield's three divisions of Northgate, Kirkgate and Westgate.

The proving of wills came under the jurisdiction of the church until 1 January 1858 when it came under secular control with the creation of the national Probate Registry. Wakefield was provided with a purpose-built probate office at the corner of King Street and Back Lane in 1863 (Figure 2).

Rates were paid variously to the Overseers of the Poor, the Surveyors of Highways, the Street Commissioners and, by nonconformists and the orthodox alike, until 1868, the Established Church. The finances needed by Quarter Sessions for county administration were collected by the High Constable of the wapentake division of Lower Agbrigg via the Overseers of the Poor. The Constable's expenses and any payment for his assistant or assistants came from a precept on the Poor Rate.

Until 1810, the Wakefield meetings of the magistrates, for both Petty and Quarter Sessions, were held at the *White Hart* which stood in Kirkgate opposite the parish church. Their Court House (sometimes referred to as the Sessions House) was the first of the public buildings to be erected in Wood Street (Figure 3). Designed by local architect Charles Watson, it was one of the first Greek Revival buildings in the country. It was built under an Act of Parliament of 1795. The original intention was to site it near the House of Correction on the west side

Figure 3: The Court House. *The author*

of the town, but the decision by the Reverend William Wood to create the new street, which was named after him, led to the change of location. It was first used, for the peripatetic Quarter Sessions, on 11 January 1810. According to *The Wakefield Star*, it had 'glaring defects', 'shew' having been studied more than 'convenience'. The paper noted that 'The magistrates are comfortably accommodated but the attorneys have scarcely room for more than half of them to sit down. The comfort of the prisoners and their keeper has been carefully consulted but the witness is placed as far as possible from the jury so that his evidence cannot be heard without excessive difficulty.' The Court House was extended in 1849-50.

The Street Commissioners
The Street Commissioners' remit covered the town from the east end of Westgate Bridge, the south side of Northgate Bar, the south end of Kirkgate Bridge (except in so far as it was the responsibility of the magistrates) and the part of the township

ANNO TRICESIMO SEXTO

Georgii III. Regis.

C A P. L.

An Act for lighting and watching the Streets, and other publick Paffages and Places, within the Town of *Wakefield*, in the County of *York*, and for more effectually cleanfing the fame, and removing and preventing Obftructions, Nuifances, and Annoyances, therein.   [24th *March* 1796.]

 HEREAS an Act of Parliament, paffed in the Eleventh Year of the Reign of His prefent Majefty, for better paving, repairing, and cleanfing, the Streets, Lanes, Alleys, and other publick Paffages and Places, within that Part of the Town of *Wakefield*, in the County of *York*, which lies within certain Limits therein defcribed, and for preventing Nuifances and Annoyances therein, and for widening and rendering the fame more commodious ; but the Provifion made by the faid Act, for cleanfing the faid Streets, Lanes, Alleys, and other publick Paffages and Places, and for removing and preventing Nuifances and Annoyances therein, is found ineffectual for thofe Purpofes, and the faid Streets, Lanes, Alleys, and other publick Paffages and Places, are not properly lighted or watched: And whereas it would be of great Benefit to the Inhabitants, and to all Perfons reforting to or travelling through the faid Town, if the feveral Streets, Lanes, Alleys, and other publick Paffages and Places, within the faid Town, were properly lighted

Preamble, recites Act 11 Geo. III.

8 N 2   and

Figure 4: An Act for lighting and watching the streets. *The author*

leading from Wrengate to Eastmoor (Figure 4). The maintenance of streets other than the principal ones was the responsibility of the Surveyors of Highways. At the turn of the century the Street Commissioners' concerns were primarily street lighting, sewering and cleansing. For this last they hired a variety of scavengers whose job was to sweep and cleanse their patch once a week and to cart away the rubbish. The Commissioners experimented briefly with taking on a man from the workhouse but this seemed to have been unsatisfactory. Separate rates were set for cleansing on the one hand, and lighting and watching on the other. The area covered by the two acts did not extend to the new housing developments of the late eighteenth and early nineteenth centuries, including St John's, Thornes Lane and the developments to the south of Kirkgate Bridge.

The Commissioners agreed to adopt new streets in the town once they were adequately paved or on the understanding that the proprietors would pay the cost of paving. George Street, formerly known just as Back Lane, for example, was adopted in 1801 from Kirkgate as far as the bottom of Market Street. Garden Street was adopted in 1806, Park Street in 1808, and Wood Street in 1809. The Commissioners bought a strip of land from the Wakefield Corn Exchange Company in 1836 in order to widen Market Street. They gradually extended the paving of the town, taking in in 1820, for example, the upper end of Warrengate.

Street flooring from early in the century was to be with Elland Edge setts as the 'bolders' or cobbles from Spurn Point were becoming scarce. Both materials were, of course, brought to Wakefield by boat. In 1834 they considered 'macadamizing' the streets but decided it would be too costly to maintain them.

The Commissioners considered building developments insofar as they might encroach on the actual streets: they might allow a bow window as it would be 'no detriment' but might require steps to a house to be removed. They were concerned if open carriage-house doors blocked the public footway. In 1801 they agreed that a Manor weighing machine, for the markets, could be placed in the street near the Manor bakehouse in Marygate. The portico on the front of the Strafford Arms was approved in 1835. In January 1836 the Commissioners agreed to Wakefield's first railway viaduct, that of the Manchester and Leeds Railway, crossing Kirkgate 'so long as it does not inconvenience waggons or foot passengers'. Once the viaduct was built, some of the Commissioners objected to it, urging that the 'piers and abutments and other obstructions' ought to be removed as being 'objectionable and dangerous' but they could not afford the expense of litigation (Figure 5). They were also concerned to compel those with property adjoining the streets to see that it had gutters and fall pipes.

The Comissioners worked under severe financial constraints. The Act of 1771 authorised them to borrow money against future income from the rates only up to £5,000. They obtained capital by seeking loans from individuals at 4% or 4.5% (advertising their need in the Leeds and, later also, the Wakefield papers) and from banks. The Act required them to have the accounts made up in June each year and to have these available for inspection by ratepayers at reasonable times

Figure 5: The original railway bridge in Kirkgate drawn by Henry Clarke in the 1880s.
Wakefield Historical Society

on payment of a shilling. Copies of their accounts were to be made available for a fee of 3d per hundred words. At times their accounts were audited externally (by, for example, Jonas Ward of the post office in 1820), at others they simply audited them themselves. There was no obligation to make them public.

Notwithstanding the assessments made for the Overseers of the Poor, a committee drawn from the Commissioners' own number at times undertook the surveying and valuing of property for their rating assessment.

The Commissioners seem to have exercised their powers less than equitably at times. In 1851 it was noted that Queen Street had only two lamps whist the parallel Market Street, where two of the Commissioners happened to live, had six.

The Commissioners, who were appointed for life, originally officially numbered 161 but recruitment to bring the number up to scratch was irregular. Although the quorum for meetings was set at a mere five, there were very many occasions when meetings had to be abandoned because fewer people were present. When this occurred, the next meeting had to be advertised by public notices which were placed on the doors of the Anglican churches and on the Market Cross itself.

Policing and keeping order

For the first half of the century, the lack of adequate policing was a perennial issue and was a significant element in the decision, ultimately, to apply for Wakefield to become a municipal corporation with the attendant duty of establishing a borough constabulary.

The watchmen, who were appointed by the Street Commissioners year by year, were on duty only at night, and for many years only in the period from the beginning of November to the end of March. In 1801 there were eight of them, one posted in Northgate, another in the Market Place (the Bull Ring), two in Kirkgate and four in Westgate. From time to time there were complaints about the men's inefficiency: they gathered, for example, in a public house to drink together when they were on duty, or they stayed in one street instead of doing the rounds. Henry Clarkson describes them as 'a flock of decrepit elderly men who were past any hard work'.

By 1833 the number of watchmen had been increased to sixteen, two of whom were superintendents. In 1835 half the number were retained throughout April. In 1839, the Commissioners determined that the watchmen must be no older than forty-five. For the first time, in 1842, when there were disturbances in Lancashire and parts of the West Riding, a number of watchmen were retained for the summer months.

Policing during the day came under the remit of the Constable, the principal officer of the town who was appointed annually (until 1830 by his predecessor) and who held a position something akin to that of a mayor. Until 1745 the town had had three Constables, one for each of the ancient wards of Kirkgate, Northgate and Westgate, but from then onwards a single individual, of some social status, was appointed.

The Constable's duties were substantial: in addition to calling public meetings when petitioned to do so by a number of inhabitants, ('requisitioned' was the customary term) he was also responsible for the execution of magistrates' warrants, the apprehension of offenders, the relief of vagrants and their removal from the town, the maintenance of the town's lock-up and pinfold and the Waver or public watering place, and, until the appointment of an inspector for the Manor, of the checking of the accuracy of weights and measures. He superintended the paid deputy, sometimes referred to as the Police Officer or Head Constable, and assistants who had the real task of maintaining law and order in the daytime.

In the first half the century, the threat of serious disturbance meant the swearing in of special constables, various ad hoc measures, and some reliance on the regular armed services, the Militia, or on bodies of volunteer infantry and cavalrymen.

The history of the Militia goes back to medieval times though there was much legislation later. Essentially, when necessary, troops were recruited by a ballot of local men who had either to serve themselves or provide a substitute. A regiment of Militia had been embodied at Wakefield on 11 February 1793 in response to the threat of local insurrection or fears of invasion from France.

The volunteer infantry and cavalrymen originated in 1894 with the Act for the Encouragement and Disciplining of Volunteer Corps. The Wakefield Volunteers Corps of Infantry was first noted in *The London Gazette* on 17 June 1794, with John Tottenham as its Major General. It seems that it divided into two classes with gentlemen members resolving to take no pay from the Government whilst a second class of Volunteers would be rewarded financially when exercising or on active duty. The former, whether or not including the latter, was listed in *The London Gazette* a year later as the Royal Wakefield Volunteers with John Tottenham promoted to the rank of Lieutenant Colonel. Volunteers were required to undertake twenty-six days' duty a year. What was probably the first serious engagement of the Volunteers came in 1796 when they helped to restore the peace during bread riots at Castleford. They were, however, disbanded in 1813 after the threat from France diminished.

No doubt Wakefield men joined one of the two regiments of West Riding Yeomanry Cavalry which were remarked in *The London Gazette* on 2 September 1794 with Earl Fitzwilliam as their Commander in Chief. A Wakefield troop was formed in 1803 as part of what was renamed the South Yorkshire Yeomanry Cavalry.

Fears of an invasion by the French led to the calling of a meeting of the inhabitants of Wakefield in November 1803 and to the setting up of a special body of constables, under the superintendence of Benjamin Heywood, who were to be called on in the event of an invasion, or of the appearance of an invasion, and to assist the county magistrates in keeping the peace. They were free to use arms if necessary.

The renewed war with France led to local groups of Volunteers taking periods of duty in neighbouring towns. In the spring of 1804 the Royal Wakefield Volunteers spent a short period in Harrogate. They were met at the parish boundary on their return home on 3 May by the Wakefield Troop of Yeomanry Cavalry with Sir Thomas Pilkington at their head. A dinner at the *White Hart* followed. The following day the Staincross Volunteers began a three-week stint in Wakefield, joined by two troops of Leeds Cavalry who were inspected on Heath Common on 6 May.

Any threat to the peace in Wakefield, however, came rather from unrest at home than from Napoleon Bonaparte. It may have been Luddite activity in Derbyshire, Leicestershire and Nottinghamshire in 1811 that led in January 1812 to a public meeting chaired by the then Constable of Wakefield, John Soulby, which resulted in the setting up of an Association Police for the remainder of the winter. Teams of volunteers were to patrol the streets each evening from 10.30pm to 5am. Watch-coats, lanterns and rattles were provided for them. The scheme seems to have been successful but came to an end in April just before an upsurge of Luddite attacks in the West Riding with threats to mill owners and actual attacks on some mills, the perpetrators most often, seemingly, to escape arrest.

Working-class rebellion in 1812 had a number of causes but central were the rising price of bread, flour and potatoes due to poor harvests, low wages, and the fear that new machinery would threaten employment. The wars with France and America severely damaged the export trade in textiles; partly to reduce costs, mill-owners installed shearing-frames which threatened the livelihood of the journeymen croppers, the skilled craftsmen who finished cloth by hand. Perhaps there were more radical underlying forces in a desire for greater Parliamentary democracy.

In March 1812 Parliament passed the Frame Breaking Act which made wilful damage to machinery or tools a capital offence.

There were local newspaper reports of the movements of troops. May 1812 saw a vast presence of troops from the Morley, Upper Agbrigg and Wakefield regiments of the local Militia, with some drunkenness and scuffles. A detachment of Royal Horse Artillery passed through Wakefield on its way to Manchester on 16 June. The Watch and Ward Act, passed on 20 March 1812, provided that every man over the age of seventeen who paid the poor rate should be ready to undertake 'the watch by night and the ward by day'. High Constables of the wapentakes were required to make lists immediately of all men covered by the Act and were to have control of special constables whose expenses, in individual townships, could be paid from the poor rate. Township constables were to make lists of everyone in their area over the age of fourteen in anticipation of violent activity.

The county's deputy lieutenants and magistrates met in Wakefield Court House on 22 June 1812, resolving that all magistrates and deputy lieutenants in the wapentakes of Agbrigg and Morley should advise Thomas Bolland, the Clerk to the general meeting of lieutenants, what number of special constables had been, or were ready to be sworn in. Members of the Royal Artillery, by then stationed in Wakefield, were reviewed on Heath Common in September. A special meeting of the Quarter Sessions on 16 September 1812, recognising that disturbances were continuing unchecked and that the 'ordinary' officers were insufficient, invoked the Watch and Ward Act. On 5 November 1812, the Wakefield Constable convened a meeting to form another association of special constables. Forty-seven volunteers were listed under the three Wakefield wards, Westgate, Kirkgate and Northgate. The Deputy Lieutenants attended at the Court House on 24 and 25 March 1813 to enrol volunteers in the Wakefield regiment of the Militia.

Wakefield itself escaped Luddite activity although Henry Clarkson recalls in his *Memories of Merry Wakefield* that his father, who had a mill at Westgate Common, on the western side of Humble Jumble Lane (now Alverthorpe Road), received a threatening letter, attached to a stone and hurled through a window. But it came close enough with the attack on James Foster's mill at Horbury on 9 April 1812. Clarkson wrote of hearing the Luddite gang tramping over Westgate Bridge on their way there. The two worst events in the West Riding were the attack on William Cartwright's Rawfolds Mill, Liversedge two days later, and the shooting of William Horsfall, a Marsden mill owner, on the night of 28 April. Quite whether he died from his wounds or the subsequent surgery it might be difficult to say but the death was treated as murder.

The man at the head of the troops deployed to put down the Luddites, Lieutenant General the Honourable Thomas Maitland, chose for a time to make Wakefield his headquarters.

For a few years the disturbances came to an end, perhaps suppressed by the harsh treatment of those who had been apprehended, or perhaps subdued by the re-opening of overseas markets, better harvests and the increasing prosperity of the textile trades.

The years immediately following the defeat of Napoleon saw lowered wages and increasing unemployment nationally. There were meetings of Radicals in London and provincial towns calling for the reform of Parliament and universal male franchise.

Fears of uprising in 1817, and an attack on the Prince Regent, led Parliament to a flurry of activity. It suspended the Habeas Corpus Act on 4 March and passed an Act against seditious assemblies which, inter alia, appeared not only to suppress meetings of more than fifty people for the purpose of inciting rebellion but also to prevent even the holding of ordinary meetings for political discussion. In January, a crowd of hundreds of working men had assembled, peacefully it appears, at the top of Westgate where a platform had been created for the event by placing two waggons together, to get up a petition for Parliamentary reform. There was an expectation of outrages on 8 June, the eve of the trial in London of supposed conspirators in organising revolution. In Yorkshire, a Government spy, William Oliver, seems to have fostered trouble: a small group of men meeting at Thornhill Lees on 8 June, including Thomas Wood, a cloth-weaver from Westgate Common, Wakefield, was surrounded by members of the Yeomanry Cavalry and brought to the Court House in Wakefield. They were subsequently released by the magistrates. Twenty-four men arrested at the same time at Huddersfield were freed at the summer Assizes in York

There were further disturbances in 1820 when, partly because of the tax on imported wool, mills were turning men off, and partly because of the privations of a severe winter. Radicals moved through Barnsley on 11 April and gathered at Grange Moor a day later where they were dispersed by the Yeomanry Cavalry. Clarkson recalls the event and observes that Grange Moor was celebrated as a rendezvous for lawless meeting of Luddites and Chartists. That week Wakefield was said to have the appearance of a military garrison. Three troops of the fourth regiment of Dragoons came from York and the Horse Artillery came from Pontefract. But *The Wakefield Journal* reported that 'the town of Wakefield and its immediate neighbourhood have preserved, during the bustle, the most complete tranquility'.

Between 1837 and 1844 there was unrest again across the North of England, in part once more due to the high price of food, in part to the level of unemployment, in part to the determination of Lancashire manufacturers to reduce the power-loom workers' wages and of Yorkshire coalmasters to lower the wages of miners, and in part to a continuing and growing desire amongst the working classes for political representation. The People's Charter, drawn up in 1838, provided one focus for insurrection. Economic depression provided a more compelling one. The worst disturbances in the West Riding came in August 1842, in what *The Leeds Mercury* described as 'the holiday insurrection', although Wakefield escaped lightly. As soon as they learned that a meeting of miners was to take place in the Music Saloon in Wood Street on 15 August, the local magistrates issued a placard, advising with regret:

> *that there are grounds for believing that a large number of persons are expected to visit Wakefield with the object of creating terror and disturbing the public peace. It is the Magistrates' intention to protect the person and property of Her Majesty's subjects from injury and danger and for that purpose they will put in force every possible means in their power authorized by law to apprehend and punish all ill doers.*

The placards invited all well disposed people to go to the Court House on the morning of the proposed meeting to be sworn in as special constables. Army pensioners under the age of sixty were required to attend at 12 noon to be sworn in. As the meeting took place, the Yeomanry Cavalry paraded the streets. Far from focusing on Chartist demands, the meeting, said to be led by 'working class miners', concentrated on the immediate problems in the coal industry. The following day, when there was 'a large gathering' of colliers in the vicinity of Wakefield, the Pontefract Yeomanry joined the Wakefield troop. There were fears the next day that a mob would seek to liberate men from Halifax and Huddersfield who had been imprisoned in Wakefield and the Cavalry pursued rioters to Horbury and Ossett where they were intent on stopping the mills and drawing the plugs on boilers. The Cavalry were sent to Huddersfield, on the night of 17 August where rioting had been prolonged for several days, and to Honley on 19 August to capture a ringleader of the mob. On Sunday, 21 August they attended the service at Huddersfield Parish Church.

Unrest in Europe in the late 1840s and 1850s, and the fear of invasion by Napoleon III, led in 1859 to the formation of the Wakefield Rifle Volunteers. In 1860 the Wakefield, Dewsbury and Goole troops were amalgamated to form one battalion. The Wakefield drill hall was built at the end of Bank Street in 1866 (Figure 6). In the 1880s it was assimilated into the King's Own Light Infantry. Some of Wakefield's leading industrialists gained their (evidently treasured) titles of 'Major' or 'Colonel' from their role in the Wakefield corps.

Fears of attacks from the Fenians (Irishmen seeking the ousting of the British Government from Ireland) three of whose number awaited execution at Manchester, led to the Home Office sending 138 men and 141 horses from the Royal Horse Artillery to Wakefield in October 1867, although they remained only for a week. (In 1871 Thomas Doyle, described as a Fenian agent, and living at Irish Row, Whitwood, was committed for trial at the Assizes for threatening to murder George Bradley of Ackton Hall after he had diverted a footpath much used by coalminers.)

The Wakefield Troop of Yeomanry continued throughout the nineteenth century, but were in the second half of the century rather to be found having field

Figure 6: The Drill Hall. *The author*

days or encampment weeks (for which members were entitled to payment), dinners or balls than taking a more active part in maintaining order. In 1844, when a second regiment was formed, the name was changed to the First West Yorkshire Yeomanry Cavalry. By 1850 the regiment had twelve troops (Wakefield men formed H Troop), normally exercising for eight days a year.

During the period of the miners' lockout in 1893 both the West Riding and Wakefield magistrates asked the Home Office for support from the army. Some fifty men from Colchester were billeted in Wakefield Town Hall. There were also a detachment of the Inniskillen Dragoons which was sent (unnecessarily, it turned out) on 16 October to Nostell Colliery where a disturbance was anticipated. There was tragedy at Featherstone when soldiers from the South Staffordshire Regiment, summoned from Bradford, fired on a mob at Ackton Hall colliery, killing two of the miners. There was much criticism subsequently that they had been overzealous and that, if only the police had not been sent to Doncaster Races, the soldiers would never have been called out.

Under the Volunteers Act of 1895, members of both the Yeomanry, by then known as the Yorkshire Dragoons, and the Wakefield Rifle Volunteers joined the regular forces to fight in South Africa in 1900. Those who returned were given the freedom of the city at ceremonies in 1901 and 1902.

Until 1848, in the more customary peaceful times, policing was left to the Street Commissioners' night watchmen and the township Constable and his assistants.

The annual vestry meetings to elect the Constable or to pass his accounts not infrequently called for retrenchment by reducing the number of assistants or reducing their wage. There was, for example, a unanimous vote in October 1827 that there should be only two assistants rather than three.

When one Shaw became the Deputy in 1812, he received 2s 6d a week. Later his salary was £50 a year but with an additional 7s 6d for every case he took for trial before the magistrates or the assizes. He had a further 5s for the apprehension of vagrants. The financial rewards for the Deputy were sufficient for at least one applicant, a Francis Dalton, to advertise his readiness to serve in the local paper. By 1836 when John Brierley was appointed, the deputy constable received £100 a year (Figure 7).

However, payment of the deputy and assistant constables became a problem in 1836 when, in accordance with the 1834 Poor Law Amendment Act, it was realised that the Poor Law Commissioners were unlikely to allow payment any longer from the Poor Rate. As anticipated, in 1838 the application for funding was rejected. A hand-wringing public meeting in October sought for ways of providing the money: should the Constable bear the burden himself? Should there be a new Improvement Bill to authorise a further rate since the Street Commissioners were restricted to paying only for night watchmen? For the first time there was the question of whether the town should seek incorporation as a municipal borough. It seemed that, as an immediate measure, the only option was to seek subscriptions and £20 was collected there and then.

Figure 7: An advertisement of 1836 for the Deputy Constable. *Wakefield MDC Cultural Services*

WANTED, an Active and Intelligent Individual for the Situation of HEAD POLICE OFFICER, in the Town of Wakefield. Salary, £100 per Annum, without any other Emoluments; he will be required to produce Certificates of Character and Ability for the Office.

Apply, if by Letter, Post-paid, to Mr. JOHN BARFF, Constable.

Wakefield, 12th May, 1836.

Concern about policing led to further requisitions to the Constable for public meetings in July and August 1839 when there had been a spate of robberies for which no one had been apprehended, and there was concern that a bill brought forward by Lord John Russell to establish rural police forces would result in Wakefield's being brought into some expensive West Riding scheme. There was criticism of the Street Commissioners and their nightwatchmen. The August meeting was convened to 'consider the propriety of an application to Parliament to repeal the present acts for the Lighting, watching and paving of the town' and it was resolved 'that the present Acts are inefficient and that new powers should be sought to seek provision for the payment of an organised local police force'. Paying a police force might be compensated by the diminution in losses from thefts since 'all the vagrants of the region seemed to prey upon Wakefield in particular'.

Lord John Russell's bill became law in 1839. It allowed, but did not compel, the Justices of the Peace to create a county force of chief and petty constables. The West Riding magistrates planned to meet on 22 September 1840 to consider their response to the Act. Meanwhile, the preceding day, Wakefield ratepayers met in the Court House. Those present warmly approved the motion of the vicar, Samuel Sharp, that 'this meeting highly approves the steps now in progress for the establishment of a local constabulary force in the Borough under their own control and management and considers it preferable in every way to a system under which they would possess insufficient control'.

When the magistrates met the following day, it was noted that they had not received a single petition in favour of their setting up a county police force. They did, however comment that the present system of parochial Constables, although sufficient for their Saxon ancestors, was not adapted to the wants of the populous districts in the West Riding. There the degree of crime was higher than should be expected in relation to the size of the population.

The Wakefield scheme came to nothing.

Intrusion from the West Riding magistrates came in 1842 as a consequence of the Act promoted by Lord Wharncliffe for the Appointment and Payment of Parish Constables. This required the magistrates to appoint constables in each township (as distinct from those presented at the Manor Court). Every able-bodied man between the ages of twenty-five and fifty-five was liable to serve except for ministers and priests, licensed victuallers, and criminals. The constables were to be unpaid except for the fees allowed for serving summonses and executing warrants. In Wakefield, for the next six years, twenty names were put forward each year from which the magistrates selected ten men.

The subsequent appointment of Constables both by the magistrates and by the Manor Court led to some confusion. At the Manor Court Leet in Wakefield in October 1842, the township Constables, who were presented in the traditional way, were told that they had no further role as 'thief-takers'. They could, however, still help to control public meetings, find billets for soldiers, and assist the Manor

Bailiff with the seizure of short weights. In 1844, for example, when Wakefield inhabitants requested a meeting to oppose the Inclosure of Heath Common, Thomas Alder, in convening it, described himself as the Chairman of Constables rather than the earlier title simply of Constable.

Men were nominated for the new role from rather lower down the social scale than those who were chosen as Wakefield's Manorial Constable – a druggist, a grocer, a gunsmith, and a tea-dealer, for example, were among the twenty names put forward in 1844. It is doubtful whether the new breed of parochial constables took their duties seriously: at the annual swearing-in in April 1847, the chairman of the bench reminded them that their position was not 'merely honorary' and that they must be prepared to discharge the duties of 'common constables'.

In 1854 the West Riding magistrates established an office and lock-up at their Court House in Wood Street to house felons taken into custody by township constables (outside Wakefield Borough) in the Wakefield petty sessional division. Correspondence was to be with the Superintending Constable, William Hall.

It was only when a further Act of Parliament was passed in 1856, making county constabularies compulsory, that the West Riding gained its police force (eight years after the Wakefield borough force had been formed). Lieutenant Colonel Charles Augustus Cobbe was appointed as the first Chief Constable in the summer of 1856 at a salary of £500. Initially the force had twenty superintendents, twenty-two inspectors, and 417 constables. Its headquarters was in Wakefield.

The Board of Guardians
The first democratically elected administration in Wakefield was that of the Board of Guardians of the Poor Law Union. Following the Poor Law Amendment Act of 1834, neighbouring parishes or townships were brought together with the aim of providing more economical and efficient administration. The Wakefield Union, which was formed in 1836 combined the townships of East Ardsley, West Ardsley, Alverthorpe with Thornes, West Bretton, Crigglestone, Emley, Flockton, Horbury, Oulton with Woodlesford, Sitlington, Sharlston, Sandal Magna, Stanley-cum-Wrenthorpe, Warmfield cum Heath, and Thorpe. Magistrates became Guardians ex officio. Wakefield people elected four further Guardians and each of the other townships was entitled to elect two more. The franchise was on a sliding scale and gave increasing numbers of votes to people of some substance; ratepayer-occupiers of property rated at less than £200 a year had one vote for each vacancy; at the other end of the scale the owners of property rated at over £400 a year had six votes per vacancy. Candidates for election had to be ratepayers occupying property rated at at least £20 a year. In theory women were able to stand but in practice they were disadvantaged by the property qualification and it was only towards the end of the century that any were elected.

The first Guardians of the Wakefield Union were elected in February 1837. In addition to the magistrates, those elected for Wakefield itself were Joshua Swallow, Thomas Tootal, George Craven and George William Harrison. From the nine candidates who had publicised their interest in the clerkship, the Guardians appointed the Wakefield solicitor John Wood Berry. The only other candidate they considered was the failed banker Thomas Rishworth.

There was some urgency in getting the Guardians elected in time for the implementation of the new provision for the registration of births, marriages and deaths, under the Act of 7 August 1836, which came into force on 1 July 1837. The new office of Registrar was created. Registration areas were those of the still-new poor law unions and the Guardians of the Poor were responsible for dividing their area into districts and for appointing a superintendent registrar for the union as a whole and, under him, further registrars for each district. The same individual might serve both as the Clerk to the Guardians and the Superintendent Registrar. In the area of the Wakefield Poor Law Union, John Wood Berry held both positions. (J W Walker notes that Berry was one of the men sworn in as a special constable in 1842 and that he met his death from an injury sustained whilst fulfilling this role.) James Holdsworth was the first Registrar for the Wakefield District. Perhaps somewhat curiously considering their role in regard to Nonconformists, two Anglican clergy were appointed to positions in other parts of the union, Thomas Flockton, the vicar of East Ardsley, and Jonathan Muncaster, vicar of Oulton.

Prior to 1837, every marriage except for those of Quakers and Jews, had to be conducted in the parish church, whether the couple were Anglicans or Dissenters. The 1836 Act for Marriages in England, passed almost immediately after the Act for Registering Births, Deaths and Marriages, changed this. Superintendent registrars were able to licence any building already registered as a place of worship so that, for the first time, Nonconformists could be married in their own chapels. Notice of the intention to marry had to be given to the registrar in advance of the wedding and either the Superintendent Registrar or the Clerk to the Guardians had to read the names at meetings of the Guardians immediately after the Minutes of the previous meeting had been dealt with. St Austin's Roman Catholic Church was one of the first Nonconformist places of worship in Wakefield to be registered for marriages, in October 1838 (Figure 8).

For a further half century the Board remained an all-male stronghold but it was the first elected body, as far as Wakefield itself was concerned, to have women sitting on it: in December 1894, Mrs Marion Dixon of Belle Vue and Mrs Anne Stubley, a Liberal who lived at Wentworth Lodge, Wakefield, and was the wife of cloth manufacturer George Stubley, joined the Board (following the Local Government Act of 1894 which had removed the property qualification.) 'Women,' *The Wakefield Express* observed, 'are peculiarly fitted to aid in the administration of the Poor Law... Girls brought up in the workhouse require the superintendence of women to ensure their better training for domestic work'.

Figure 8: St Austin's Church. *The author*

Wakefield becomes a Municipal Borough

Wakefield became a municipal borough, with elected councillors, in 1848 under the 1835 Municipal Corporations Act. Whilst Leeds had obtained its charter of incorporation back in 1662, Sheffield was the first town in the West Riding to take advantage of the Act, in 1843. Bradford followed in 1847. Halifax petitioned for the application of the act at much the same time as Wakefield. (Among other nearby towns, Dewsbury was incorporated in 1862, Huddersfield in 1868, and Barnsley in 1869)

Prior to 1848, some of the town's business was brought up at (quite numerous) ad hoc public meetings following a requisition to the Constable. These might well lead to a resolution for some kind of action and the setting up of a committee. It was a form of democracy. Before the magistrates built the Court House, meetings were usually held in the Manorial Moot Hall just off Kirkgate. The matter of such meetings might be quite trivial or of considerable moment. At the beginning of the century, the war with France was of major concern for Wakefield's industries. Duly requisitioned, the Constable convened a meeting in the Moot Hall on 30 January 1801 at which it is was agreed to petition the King for peace on the grounds that, with most of the ports of Europe closed to British Trade, 'most of the industrious and laborious families' were sinking into poverty and the poor rate locally, and taxes nationally, had increased. Yorkshire's

Members of Parliament, William Wilberforce and Henry Lascelles, were to be asked to present the petition to the king. In 1815 a public meeting determined to petition Parliament against any increased tax on imported corn. In 1832, the Constable was required to call a meeting to pursue a proposal for a memorial to the Reverend Thomas Rogers who had been the afternoon lecturer at the parish church . In 1834 John Barff, constable of the day, called a meeting in support of the Manchester and Leeds Railway Bill at which it was resolved that 'the wealth and importance of the large and populous district between Leeds and Sheffield needs every facility for the transport of goods and people'. In May 1842 the Constable was required to call a meeting to raise subscriptions to relieve the suffering caused at Hamburg by the great fire of 5 May which destroyed a third of the city. The committee received £245. There were many more such gatherings. Following Wakefield's incorporation, townspeople called similarly on the Mayor. There was, for example, a requisitioned public meeting in February 1852 following the bursting of the Bilberry Reservoir above Holmfirth in order to establish a relief fund.

Dissatisfaction with policing played a substantial part in the moves to seek incorporation for Wakefield. The Streets Commissioners themselves admitted in 1847 that there was a failure to coordinate the work of the night watchmen and the daytime police and that this contributed to the failure to pursue robbers. But a more general dissatisfaction with the nature and achievements of the Streets Commissioners was a regular theme at public meetings in the 1830s and 40s. Thomas Micklethwaite, proprietor of *The Wakefield Journal*, regularly campaigned from the mid 1840s via editorials for better local government.

The Street Commissioners had no powers for paving, lighting and watching what were by then some of the most populous parts of the town. Whilst the inhabitants of those areas enjoyed the benefits the Commissioners brought to the town itself, they paid nothing whatever towards these. It was urged, too, that the Street Commissioners Acts were unjust, and certainly undemocratic, in that they provided for a body of men to tax others who had no opportunity to vote for them.

In 1846-7 the Commissioners toyed with seeking an Improvement Act which would extend the boundaries of their province and would give them responsibility for the daytime police and for the fire engines.

The first moves in Wakefield to petition the Privy Council for incorporation seem to have come when Thomas Micklethwaite, who was refusing to pay the rates due to the Street Commissioners, wrote in *The Wakefield Journal* about the kind of administration that was really needed. The Constable, John Flatman, was requested to call a public meeting which took place in the Court House on 21 April 1847. Micklethwaite asked the meeting whether the ratepayers 'were satisfied with the old women wending their way up that spiral staircase and assembling in the market house or old-fashioned chamber and who knew as much about business as he knew about flying to the moon'. The decision to seek incorporation was a controversial one, many believing that a new Improvement Act would have been adequate. But the day was carried. The Charter of Incorporation was granted on 15 March 1848, providing for a Mayor, eight aldermen and twenty-four councillors.

Despite the hopes of some local people, the election for the first council rapidly became a party affair. A Ratepayers' Association was formed, ostensibly to nominate the best men in the town but effectively to secure the election of Tories. The Whigs and Radicals, under the Liberal banner, nominated their men. At the election on 12 May, only one of the seven wards – St John's – returned Ratepayers' candidates so that twenty-one of the twenty-four new councillors were Liberals or Radicals. The cornfactor George William Harrison, long a Radical activist and one of the first men elected to the Board of Guardians, was elected as Mayor and, following the first annual election in November 1848, was chosen as Mayor for a further twelve months. James Whitham, a local lawyer who had handled the petition for the Charter, was appointed as the first (part-time) Town Clerk.

The new council immediately appointed a Watch Committee and one of this body's first decisions, when it met on 23 May 1848, was to establish a police force. James McDonnold, who was an Inspector with the Manchester Police, was appointed as the Chief Constable. His salary was £130. Another applicant for the post, James Aubrey Chipstead, who had been superintendent of the Street Commissioners' night watchmen, was appointed with the rank of Superintendent at a salary of £60 and was sometimes still referred to as the 'superintendent of the night police. He succeeded McDonnold in 1868. (He was encouraged to retire in 1877 on the grounds that he was too old to cope with the work. He died in 1908!) There were, additionally, two Inspectors and sixteen constables. The force began active work on 4 September 1848 operating from the building in King Street which had previously been used by the township constables and the vagrant master. The constables each had a 'beat' which was expected to take between forty and sixty minutes to patrol. McDonnold was to deal with all police matters when they came before the magistrates at the Court House and he and one of the inspectors would patrol the streets at night. The practice of keeping the perquisites as a part of the salary was abolished and any sums coming in this way were to be contributed to the Borough Fund. During the daytime, McDonnold was to patrol the 'principal thoroughfares' and to make spot checks on the constables. For some years the police served also as the fire brigade manning a single borough engine.

In January 1849, the Council determined to extend street lighting to the new areas of Wakefield, which were not under the jurisdiction of the Street Commissioners, at Westgate Common and Eastmoor.

The new Council's numerous bye laws (there were in fact initially eighty-two of them), although no doubt largely drawing on model byelaws devised elsewhere, give some indication of the range of problems vexing inhabitants.

There were, for example, fines for allowing chimneys to catch fire, allowing cattle to wander in the streets, carrying uncovered carcasses through the streets, allowing carriages to stand in the streets unnecessarily, organising dog or cock fights, and exhibiting indecent books or singing obscene songs. Prostitutes were forbidden from importuning.

The Council appointed a sanitary committee in 1848 but the Council's own powers to influence the sanitary condition of the town were, effectively, nil. McDonnold was required to act as the Inspector of Nuisances but had no authority to enforce action.

Some of the first councillors, including Harrison, were ambitious for the town. An Improvement Bill was suggested in January 1849 to repeal the Acts which had given powers to the Street Commissioners, and to enable the Corporation to purchase the gas, water and Borough Market companies and the Manorial rights of fairs and markets. A few months later the Parliamentary Committee was asked to seek an Improvement Bill allowing the authority to drain and cleanse the streets and to provide a cemetery. A year later it was bent on securing a separate Commission of the Peace for the town. Before the end of the century, all but one of the goals had been achieved.

By 1851 the number of Street Commissioners had dwindled to forty-eight, only thirty-two of whom were resident in the Wakefield township. Its Acts of 1771 and 1796 were wholly inadequate by the middle of the century and its powers were limited to the township, thus excluding parts of the Borough. At a public meeting in April 1851, those present made it clear that they wanted the Council to have the additional role of a Board of Health rather than simply pursue a new Improvement Act. The Corporation applied for this power and, as a preliminary, an Inspector, William Ranger, was sent by the General Board of Health to hold an Inquiry into the sanitary condition of the borough. The Council's Sanitary Committee, the Chief Constable, a number of local doctors, and many other individuals provided him with evidence.

Ranger's report was a horrific indictment of the state of the town. It had bad drainage, defective scavenging, and a scanty water supply. It showed that the Street Commissioners dealt actively with only three and a half miles of the fifteen and a half miles of streets in the Borough. The Highways Surveyors of Stanley cum Wrenthorpe and Alverthorpe with Thornes were responsible for four and a half miles. The remaining seven and a half miles were no one's responsibility other than the property owners. The West Riding magistrates were responsible for the bridges. A scavenger who gave evidence said that Pincheon Street was swept once a year; Providence Street was swept twice a year but, although it was within the province of the Street Commissioners, they had no interest in it because none of its inhabitants was a ratepayer; other streets, which had not been adopted, were never swept at all.

The Act of Parliament confirming the Corporation's powers as a Board of Health was passed in May 1853, at last doing away with the Street Commissioners.

At a meeting on 23 May both the Street Commissioners and the Surveyors of Highways formally relinquished their responsibilities within the Borough. The Council immediately established a Board of Works Committee to deal with sewers, drains, ditches, becks, streets and highways, and an Improvement Committee to make sure that all streets were named and properly numbered, to consider improving the line of streets and to deal with obstructions. James Whitham became Clerk to the Board of Health at an increased salary of £300. Rather than immediately appoint a Borough Surveyor, the Council appointed a local man, William Clarkson, as Clerk of Works at £130. Two years later Clarkson was replaced by Matthew Ogle Tarbotton at the same salary but with the title of Surveyor A local butcher, Joseph Johnson, was appointed Inspector of Lodging Houses, Slaughter Houses and Nuisances.

For many years Council meetings were held in the Court House in Wood Street, or in the Public Rooms which had been erected in Wood Street in 1821-3. Committee meetings were generally held in Barstow Square in offices rented from Charles Barstow. Councillors would have liked to build a Town Hall but financing it was a daunting problem especially when there was strong opposition by the ratepayers to any 'unnecessary' expense. In 1854, with the intention of providing a Town Hall, the Corporation acquired the 'old croft' a plot of land in Wood Street which had formerly been a quarry, from widow Elizabeth Briggs. Her husband, Isaac, had levelled the land and intended to open a vegetable market there but was prevented under the terms of the Borough Market Company's charter. A competition was held for designs, with a £50 prize, which was won by G T Robinson of Leamington. On 21 June the Council determined to seek approval from the General Board of Health to 'mortgage the rates' for the new building. Reaction, when the decision was reported in the local press, was marked. Just as in the past ratepayers had 'requisitioned' the Constable to hold a public meeting, now 1144 of them requested the Mayor to do so. On 10 July, at the Court House, at a meeting chaired by Edward Sykes (as the Mayor, declaring his support for the scheme, declined to preside), there was a near unanimous vote opposing the Council's decision. The arguments against it ranged from the depressed state of trade, the high taxation because of the war with Russia, the high price of food, the legacy of debt from the Street Commissioners which the ratepayers had to finance, the cost of buying the Manorial Soke rights, which again still had to be met, to the more pressing need for adequate drainage and sewerage and the possibility that the Corporation would buy and extend the water undertaking. Although the Council was anxious to secure an independent Commission of the Peace for the town for which a court-room and offices would be needed, it was argued that it was not necessary to do so.

The following year, when the Public Rooms in Wood Street came on the market, the Council considered buying them. As late as 1861, still unwilling to commit itself to a new Town Hall, the Council took a ten-year lease of premises in Crown Court which were owned by Jonathan Bayldon and had recently been

Figure 9: The Old Town Hall. *The author*

very substantially damaged by fire, for use as a Council Chamber, committee rooms and offices (Figure 9) Its first meeting in the so-called Town Hall was on 9 November 1861.

It was a short-sighted step. The lack of an adequate Town Hall was one of the chief reasons why, when separate Assizes for the West Riding were established in 1864, this important and economically advantageous function, generally expected to come to Wakefield, was located instead in Leeds.

Women who were ratepayers were entitled to vote in Local Government elections from 1869. In the November election of that year the candidates' election addresses began for the first time with the words 'Ladies and Gentlemen'.

Wakefield obtained a separate Commission of the Peace in 1870 although for some years prior to that separate Wakefield sessions had been conducted by the Mayor and ex-Mayor under the aegis of the West Riding. The first magistrates were sworn in, eight of them Liberal and four Tory, on 23 March in the small court at the Court House which Wakefield was to use for the next decade. W S Banks, later the author of *Walks about Wakefield* (1871), was appointed as the first Clerk of the Peace.

Eventually, in 1875, in a period when the Tories had a majority on the Council, the Corporation bought the Tammy Hall, lying between Back Lane and the George and Crown Yard, and demolished a part of it to allow for a Town Hall to be built on both the Wood Street plot and the newly-cleared site. What was left of the Tammy Hall was converted into premises for Wakefield's police and fire brigade (Figure 10). The architect for the alterations was G H France. A tunnel was begun to allow prisoners to be taken directly to cells in the Town Hall whenever it was built.

Figure 10: The Fire Station of 1878. *The author*

The Wakefield Improvement Act of 1877 authorised the building of the Town Hall. A new competition was held for its design. The scheme of the London-based T E Colcutt was chosen from some thirty schemes, and the Town Hall was built between 1877 and 1880 (Figure 11). The foundation stone was laid on 18 October 1877. The clock, designed by the Leeds firm of William Potts and Son, was installed and set in motion at the beginning of September 1880. The same firm had built the clock at Westgate Station in June of that year. The Town Hall was formally opened on 18 October, most Wakefield businesses giving their workpeople a half day holiday (Figure 12) It had a splendid panelled court room and, immediately below it, three cells from which steps led down to the tunnel (Figures 13 and 14).

The election of 1893 saw Wakefield gain its first Labour councillor, Thomas Broadhead. He represented Calder Ward. The vote was tied but the returning officer, a Liberal, chose Broadhead in preference to the Conservative candidate.

The municipal borough was extended in 1895 to take in a small part of Stanley

Figure 11: The Town Hall. *Yorkshire Archaeological Society*

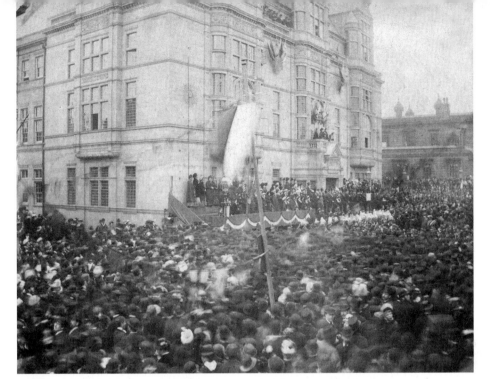

Figure 12: The opening of the Town Hall in 1880. *The John Goodchild Collection*

Figure 13: The Court Room. *The author*

Figure 14: The cells beneath the Court Room. *The author*

cum Wrenthorpe and of Alverthorpe with Thornes. Most of Alverthorpe was added to the Municipal borough in 1900, initially electing three liberals to the Council. It was not until 1909 that Sandal and Belle Vue became part of the municipal borough.

The diminution of Manorial powers

The obligation of inhabitants of the Manor to take their corn and malt for grinding at the lord's mill went back to medieval times. Originally the mills provided a useful service but by the nineteenth century the system was much

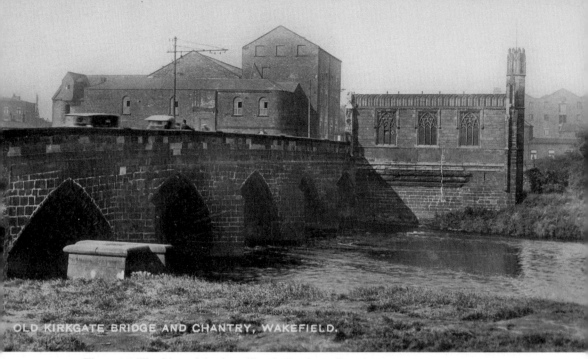

OLD KIRKGATE BRIDGE AND CHANTRY, WAKEFIELD.

Figure 15: The Manorial soke mill, rebuilt after a fire of 1872. *The Friends of Wakefield Chantry Chapel.*

resented as a restriction on free trade (Figure 15). William Ranger, in his report on the Sanitary Condition of Wakefield, noted that, since the lessees sold flour of varied quality, the poor were tempted to buy the cheaper, but bad, flour. There was resentment, too, that neither the owners nor the tenants of the mill paid rates either to the Overseers of the Poor or to the Street Commissioners. There was an attempt in 1828 to quash the soke but its legality was upheld at the Assizes in York. The high price of flour, regarded as a tax on food, was among the factors said to be holding back Wakefield's economic development, preventing growth in the baking, confectionery and brewing trades although it was also argued, in 1851, that the ready availability of the milling contributed to Wakefield's 'present improved condition'. Between 1817 and 1851 some sixty people, including corn merchants, beerhouse keepers, inkeepers and retailers paid compensation to the soke lessees for infringements. To provide employment for prisoners, corn was ground at the Wakefield House of Correction between 1823 and 1842 but the magistrates paid the soke lessees an annual sum for the concession. The people of Ossett were discharged legally from the soke, by paying compensation, in 1832. In 1849 a group styled the Wakefield Free Trade and Economic Flour Association set about challenging the soke by setting up shops for the sale of flour bought elsewhere at a penny less than the price charged by the soke mills. George Parkin recalled at a meeting of the Wakefield Paxton Society in 1908 that his father was persuaded to defy the soke and to sell flour unlawfully at his shop at the bottom of Cheapside (Figure 16). Following a test case at York Assizes in March 1851, where the soke rights were upheld, a group of individuals, seemingly led by the cornfactor Richard Dunn, formed themselves into a committee to bring about the demise of the soke rights by purchase. By that time the mills were in the ownership of Philip Bennett the younger, son-in-law of Sir Thomas Pilkington. They had been leased since 1843 by the two sons of Jose Luis Fernandes, Nowell Luis Fernandes and Jose Luis Fernandes the younger. The Mayor was requested to hold a public meeting for the inhabitants not only of the Wakefield township but of the neighbouring townships of Alverthorpe with Thornes, Crigglestone, Horbury, Sandal, and Stanley cum Wrenthorpe. A formal committee was established to carry the business forward. The Fernandes brothers expressed their willingness (if suitably compensated) to have the soke abolished. An Act of Parliament was sought only after agreement had been reached to abandon the actions against infringers. The £18,000 cost was to be borne by an ad hoc rate collected over a period of six years from the six townships involved. On the passing of the Act, twenty-five trustees representing the six townships (the

> **WAKEFIELD SOKE.**
>
> *PUBLIC NOTICE.*
>
> WE, the undersigned JOHN FORGE, Agent to PHILIP BENNET, the younger, Esquire, the proprietor of the WAKEFIELD SOKE MILLS, and NOWELL LUIS FERNANDES and JOSE LUIS FERNANDES, the younger, Lessees of the said Soke Mills do hereby give NOTICE, that any person or persons who shall, or may hereafter open any house, shop, or other premises for the the sale of flour, meal, or malt, to any resiant or inhabitant for consumption within the precincts of the said Soke, and which flour, meal, or malt has not been ground at the said Soke Mills, will be immediately restrained by an order of the Court of Chancery; and legal proceedings will be instituted against all parties purchasing for consumption within the precincts of the said Soke, any flour, meal, or malt not ground at the said Soke Mills.
>
> Dated at Wakefield this 13th day of March 1850.
>
> JOHN FORGE } Agent to Philip Bennet, the younger, Esquire, the Proprietor of the Soke Mills
>
> N. L. FERNANDES, } Lessees of the
> J. L. FERNANDES, } said Mills.

Figure 16: A notice of 1850 warning against the infringement of the soke. *Wakefield MDC Cultural Services*

Wakefield ones included corn millers and corn merchants) were appointed to put it into operation. The ending of the Soke rights on 31 December 1853 brought widespread celebrations. At the *Swan with Two Necks* in Westgate in January 1854, a sheep was roasted whole, with coal donated by the New Victoria Colliery Company. A week later the Infant School at Thornes was used for a feast which included sheep roasted by the *Commercial* and *Bishop Blaise Inns*. A malt kiln at the premises of corn miller James Fawcett was converted into a banqueting hall for a work-force of thirty-five. The Soke Mill itself (sometimes called the Custom Mill) was sold in 1870 to the Aire and Calder Navigation. The sale included mills on either side of the river, amongst them a saw mill, bone mill and cloth-fulling mills, together with the boat-builder's yard adjoining the cloth-fulling mills.

The Manor jurisdiction in regard to the recovery of debts ceased in 1847 when County Courts were established for this purpose. The authority of the Manor over the town's markets was ceded to the Borough Market Company again in 1847.

Although Wakefield's foremost townsman was, from 1848, the Mayor, the Manor Court Leet continued to appoint a Head Constable until Richard Everington Goldthorpe was appointed in October 1885. Probably his sole remaining task was to serve as chairman of the jury when the Courts Leet heard charges against traders who had false weights and inaccurate balances. He was in the 1880s sometimes referred to as the High Constable of the Manor. No new Constable was chosen in 1886 or, as far as is known, thereafter, and Goldthorpe led the jury that October and for several subsequent years, certainly until 1890.

The Manorial right to check and stamp weights and measures and to fine those whose equipment was inaccurate continued until 1892 when Wakefield and other affected local authorities joined with the West Riding County Council to buy the rights.

The Manor retained its rights in regard to copyhold land until the principle of copyhold tenure was formally abolished for new conveyances in 1926. All remaining copyhold transactions were completed by 1936.

Representation in Parliament
Until 1832, Wakefield was represented in Parliament by the two county members for Yorkshire. Contested elections were rare, partly at least because of the vast expense candidates had to bear. But 1807 saw the first contested election in sixty-six years with William Wilberforce, who had just led the successful campaign for the abolition of the slave trade, vying with Charles William Wentworth, then styled Lord Milton, who had only just come of age, and with Henry Lascelles of Harewood House. Earl Fitzwilliam and the Earl of Harewood, the heads of two great county families, spent some £100,000 each in promoting their sons' campaigns. Those entitled to vote (male freeholders whose property was valued at at least forty shillings a year) had to travel to York to cast their vote. Thirteen booths were erected in the Castle yard, each designated for the men from specific wapentakes, and the election took place over fifteen days in June and July. (The previous poll, in 1741, had taken eight days.) The published poll book shows that many Wakefield voters, although allowed two votes, chose only the Whig, Lord Milton. Milton and Wilberforce were elected. Lord Milton continued as one of the members for Yorkshire until 1830. Wilberforce relinquished his seat in 1812 whereupon Lascelles succeeded him.

There was strong support in Wakefield for the Reform bills of 1831 and 1832. Perhaps since *The Wakefield Journal* was at that time a staunchly liberal paper there are few reports of any anti-reform movement. Following requisitions to the Constable, pro-Reform meetings were held in February and March 1831 with a petition sent to Lord Morpeth, then one of Yorkshire's members of Parliament. Radicals raised the questions of universal male suffrage and the secret ballot but these reforms found no place in the petitions. The carriages carrying pro-reform candidates for Yorkshire seats at the general election of 1831 were taken in procession from the gates of Thornes House to a hustings set up in Westgate in a procession headed by a trumpeter and bands, followed by men from the principal trades of the town with banners flying. Such was the public enthusiasm that the horses were taken from the shafts and people themselves drew the carriages. Anticipating the passing of the Reform Act, Wakefield people petitioned Daniel Gaskell in August 1831 to stand in the expected election for the new borough. Lord Wharncliffe's opposition to reform led to his being burned in effigy, dressed in the uniform of the Yorkshire Hussars in the Market Place in October 1831.

The passing of the Reform Act was marked in Wakefield by festivities in August 1832 with a procession, led by the Constable on horseback, from the new Parliamentary borough boundary at Cross Lane to the Market Place, and a dinner which, to accommodate the vast numbers, had to be spread across twenty-six inns.

The Parliamentary borough boundaries were rather wider than those of the township, taking in a part of the Stanley cum Wrenthorpe and Alverthorpe with Thornes townships (Figure 17).

Only those ratepayers who had occupied houses valued at £10 (or more) a year for at least the previous twelve months were entitled to vote in the new borough elections. In Wakefield this meant that 722 men out of a population of almost 16,000 were qualified. Many people who had had the vote previously for county elections as £2 freeholders were excluded from

Figure 17: Map showing the Parliamentary Borough boundaries. *The author's collection*

voting in Wakefield. However, the 1832 Reform Act gave the West Riding its own county representation, with two members of Parliament. Holders of forty-shilling freehold property within the Borough who did not actually occupy it were still entitled to vote for the West Riding members. Some few who were both £2 freeholders and occupiers of a different £10 property, had dual voting rights. At the first contested election for a West Riding member, in 1835, 163 people with property in the Wakefield township were entitled to vote.

There were schemes to persuade T O Gasgoigne of Parlington Hall, and James Milnes Gaskell of Thornes House to stand for the Wakefield seat but in the event Daniel Gaskell was the only candidate. Gaskell was re-elected in 1835 when he polled 278 votes against the 221 registered for the Tory candidate, Hon William Sebright Lascelles. Two years later the position was reversed and Lascelles gained 307 votes against the 281 cast for Gaskell. James Milnes Gaskell was elected for Much Wenlock.

Whilst in 1837 the election for the Wakefield member of Parliament passed peacefully enough, the nomination day for the West Riding candidates saw a riot in Wood Street in which two people were killed. Thousands of people with adherence to both parties had gathered in Wood Street to hear the nomination speeches. The Tories stood close to the *Woodman Hotel* on the east whilst the

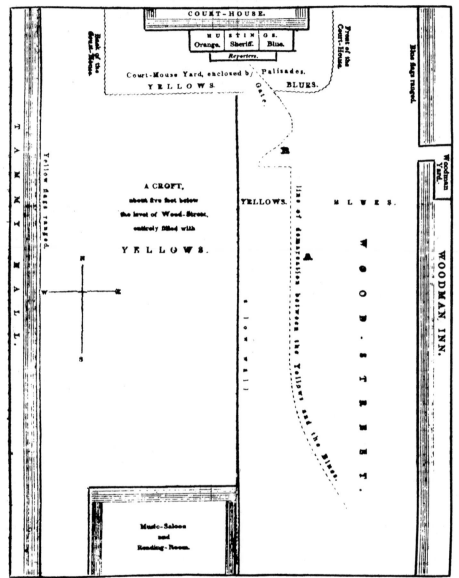

Figure 18: Plan from *Tle Leeds Mercury* showing the positions of the supporters of the two parties at the time of the riot. *Wakefield MDC Cultural Services*

Whigs and Radicals occupied the west side of the street and, in particular, the vacant land between the Court House and the Public Rooms. Surging forward some of the 'blues' had formed a wedge amongst the 'yellow and oranges' when a small force of yellows, armed with sticks, marched up Wood Street and tried to drive the 'blues' from the midst of the yellows, seeking weapons from stable yards and tearing down the railings in front of the Court House itself. Margaret Moore, a charwoman from Leeds, there presumably just to enjoy the spectacle, suffered a fractured skull when she was struck by a brick. She died a week later in Leeds Infirmary. The Constable, John Barff, read the Riot Act, but in a hail of slates and further bricks, a second fatality occurred when William Carter of Flushdyke Mill, Ossett, was struck down (Figure 18).

The actual polling took place later in the week and the Whig candidates, Lord Morpeth and Sir George Strickland were elected in preference to the Tory, John Stuart Wortley. The inquests on both the victims found a verdict of manslaughter against a person or persons unknown.

When at the 1841 General Election, the Liberal Joseph Holdsworth, of the Belle Isle Dyeworks, was elected for Wakefield by a majority of twenty-eight, the Tories petitioned Parliament on the grounds that, as the Returning Officer, Holdsworth was actually ineligible. Lascelles replaced him.

A Wakefield Conservative Association was founded in February 1845 to rally support for future Tory candidates.

In 1852, when George Sandars was elected for a second term, the riot act had again to be read and members of the 4th Dragoons, billeted at the *Graziers Arms* on Oakenshaw Road, were put on stand-by. Thomas Avison, a whitesmith of Thornes Lane, was taken captive by four local men and hustled away by coach to Clayton West where he was held in an inn and plied with drink until the poll had closed. He brought a claim for assault but the sole consequence was that the men were each fined £1.

The worst possible situation for Wakefield resulted from the 1859 election when the colliery owner, J C D Charlesworth, stood for the Tories and W H Leatham, a banker, of Hemsworth Hall, stood in the Liberal interest. It was a close call. Leatham was returned by 406 votes to Charlesworth's 403. The Tories promptly alleged corruption and a Parliamentary Commission of inquiry was appointed. Its report, published in 1860, makes sensational reading and is an indictment of both parties: both candidates spent vast sums in bribes, the supporters of each were guilty of intimidation. A worsted manufacturer, Abraham Lupton of Snow Hill, was kidnapped by Charlesworth's allies to prevent his attending the poll. Leatham was unseated and the borough writ was suspended leaving Wakefield without Parliamentary representation at a highly critical time for the town when Leeds Members of Parliament were lobbying to secure the West Riding Assizes for Leeds. John Barff Charlesworth, who had served as the election agent for his Tory cousin, was imprisoned.

In the wake of the 1860 debacle, a new Conservative Association and a Liberal

Association were formed. The latter's constitution included rules for ward committees and the injunction to 'keep your eye on the Tory and undecided voters and try to find a defect to get them off the register'!

Disraeli's 1867 Reform Act gave the vote to substantial numbers of the working class. It extended the franchise to all male householders in the borough and to lodgers paying more than £10 a year in rent. This brought the Wakefield electorate up to almost 4,000 although by now the population stood at some 28,000. Anxious to woo the new voters, Wakefield Tories set up the Wakefield Working Men's Conservative Association in 1867.

The next election on 18 November 1868, seems to have passed peacefully enough. It again demonstrated the very close support in Wakefield for both parties, the Liberal candidate, Somerset Beaumont of Bretton Hall, gaining the seat by a majority of only 39 with 1558 votes compared with the 1519 cast for the Tory candidate Thomas Kemp Sanderson.

The secret ballot was introduced nationally in 1872 but, although voting was no longer a public affair and the rowdyism seems largely to have gone, bribery still remained a problem. In February 1874, the Tory Edward Green was elected by 1779 votes to the 1600 cast for the Liberal Robert Bownas Mackie. Following a Liberal petition, the charge of corruption was heard at the Court House in April. Witnesses spoke of assignations at public houses such as the *Black Horse* and of being handed substantial sums of money – 30s or £2 – to vote for Green. Judge Groves pointed out that, whilst there was 'not the slightest personal imputation' against Green, there had certainly been illegal activities in his camp and, in particular, a number of unauthorised committee rooms had been set up. One was at the church school in Zetland Street where a 'committee room' opened directly onto the room with the polling booths. The judge declared the election void. A new writ was issued and in May Sanderson was elected for the Tories with a handsome majority of almost 2,000. However, in 1880 the pendulum swung again and Robert Bownas Mackie became Wakefield's member of Parliament until his death in 1885. In the subsequent general elections Wakefield continued to elect Conservative/Unionist candidates for the remainder of the century. The Parliamentary Borough boundaries were extended in 1885 to include the Belle Vue area. How far this contributed to the Conservative success can be only a matter of speculation. In fact in 1900 Viscount Milton was returned for the Conservatives unopposed. However voters in the new Normanton consituency, which included Alverthorpe, Horbury, Outwood, Sandal and Stanley, elected Ben Pickard the miners' leader on a Liberal/Labour platform, in November 1885. He had a firm majority at all succeeding elections until his death in 1904.

Women were not entitled to vote for the national government in the nineteenth century but, certainly by the end of the century, they were not inactive politically. The Wakefield branch of the Primrose League, was formed by women for women in February 1886 under the leadership of Mary Green, wife of the industrialist and some-time Wakefield member of Parliament, Edward Green. It was named the 'Dr Primrose Habitation' after the eponymous character in Goldsmith's *The Vicar of Wakefield*. The League was a Conservative association aiming to protect the Established Church, the Crown and the Conservative Party, founded in 1883 and was named after Benjamin Disraeli's favourite flower. Its ideal was to bridge the gap between 'the two nations', the rich and the poor and to form one great Conservative nation. To this end the Conservative Party set out to win the adherence of the newly enfranchised working men and succeeded in doing this until the Liberal landslide of 1906. The Primrose League played a considerable part in that success, fostering working-class support by providing social activities and entertainment.

Wakefield becomes the seat of the West Riding County Council
Following the 1888 Local Government Act, the West Riding County Council came into existence, taking over many of the administrative responsibilities that had formerly lain with the magistrates. Although Wakefield had been *de facto* the county town of the West Riding for centuries, there was no certainty that the new Council would make it the centre of its administration. Leeds was a strong contender. Both towns were readily accessible by road and rail. But the magistrates had bought Rishworth House with substantial land, in Wood Street in 1877 and the Council made the decision in 1892 to build its County Hall on the site. Rishworth House had been built for Thomas Rishworth but was bought in 1872 by Samuel Whitham the ironfounder. The design for the new county hall was opened to competition with the indication that something in the Queen Anne

Figure 19: The County Hall in the 1890s. *Yorkshire Archaeological Society*

or Renaissance style would be appreciated. The competition was won by the London-based architects, James Gibson and Samuel Russell and the main building contract went to Armitage and Hodgson of Leeds. Although the architects had planned gas lighting, the Council took the bold decision of having electricity instead, doubtless knowing that Wakefield Corporation would shortly be able to provide the supply. County Hall, the last of the great buildings of the nineteenth century, was opened by Charles George Milnes Gaskell on 22 February 1898 (Figure 19). On its Bond Street frontage it has a colonnade of seven niches, each of which formerly contained a statue representing the county's industries, coalmining, ironfounding, spinning, glass-blowing, agriculture, engineering and pottery.

Sources

An Act for discharging the inhabitants of the townships of Wakefield, Alverthorpe with Thornes, Stanley cum Wrenthorpe, Sandal Magna and Crigglestone from the custom of grinding corn, grain and malt at certain corn mills in the said townships and for making compensation to the proprietors. 6 Victoria xxvii.

West Riding Magistrates' Quarter Sessions Order Books.

Wakefield Street Commissioners Order Books.

Henry Clarkson, *Memories of Merry Wakefield*.

John Goodchild, 'The Constables and Town Officials of Wakefield', Wakefield Historical Society Journal, Volume 13, 2004.

Ian F W Beckett, *The Amateur military tradition 1558-1945*, 1991

Anthony Dawson, 'Wakefield Rifle Volunteers', *Aspects of Wakefield 2*, 1999.

An Act for the more effective preservation of the peace by enforcing the duties of watching and warding. 52 George III xvii.

Colin Jackson, *Wakefield Constabulary 1848-1968*, 1983.

Beatrice and Sydney Webb, *Parish and County*, 1906.

Robert Reid, *The Land of Lost Content*, 1986

An Act for more effectively preventing seditious meetings and assemblies. 57 George III.

David Johnson, *Regency Revolution: The Case of Arthur Thistlewood*, Salisbury, 1974.

An Act for the Appointment and Payment of Parish Constables, 5 and 6 Victoria CIX.

William Ranger, *Report to the General Board of Health on a preliminary inquiry into the sewerage, drainage and supply of water, and the sanitary condition of the inhabitants of the borough of Wakefield, 1852.*

Kate Taylor, 'How the Assizes came to Leeds', in Wakefield Historical Society Journal, Volume 13, 2004.

Keith Cowlard, 'The Urban development of Wakefield 1801-1901', unpublished thesis presented to the University of Leeds Department of Geography, 1974.

Wakefield Liberal Association constitution (undated but of the 1860s).

$\mathscr{2}$ $\mathscr{A}$MENITIES

Most of the amenities taken for granted in Wakefield today were developed in the nineteenth century, the changes mirroring the wider, national picture. During our period the first Wakefield newspapers were published, the town gained a gas supply, eventually a good, fresh water supply and, by the end of the century, its own electricity generating station. Again by the end of the century it had a general hospital, a specialist fever hospital, a county hospital for those with psychiatric illnesses, and a new hospital at the workhouse. The needs of the poor were addressed in many ways.

Provision for the sick and the poor

In 1787 Wakefield saw the beginnings of a local health service when the General Dispensary was founded in a small house at the bottom of Northgate. The Overseers of the Poor allotted it £30 a year. Otherwise it was largely dependent on subscription. Its original home was pulled down in the early 1820s and the Dispensary moved to the basement of the then new Public Rooms in Wood Street. Here there was residential accommodation for the apothecary and for two house-servants in what was described in 1832 as 'a poor miserable underground apartment contiguous to a damp beer and porter cellar'. The death of the apothecary, Thomas Hodgson, attributed in part to his poor living conditions, led to the move to a house in Barstow Square. The subscribers determined at their annual meeting in 1840 to seek the means of creating 'a few wards' for admitting people requiring surgery. In 1853 the Dispensary moved again to a house in Wood Street and in 1854, after a generous donation from Thomas Clayton, the scheme to build wards came to fruition. The name was changed to the Wakefield Dispensary and Clayton Hospital (Figure 20). Clayton, whose fortune had come from tallow chandlery, was one of the first aldermen of the new municipal corporation. The death of Prince Albert in 1861 added a memorial wing. Clayton died in 1868 leaving half his estate, as much as £600 a year to the Hospital. In 1876-9 a new hospital was erected to designs, chosen in a competition, by William Bakewell of Leeds (Figure 21). A two-storey extension at the Wentworth Street end of the building, was opened in November 1900. It was provided by Mrs Louisa Milnes Gaskell in memory of her husband, Colonel Milnes Gaskell of Lupset Hall, and had two wards for children. Among fund-raising efforts was 'Hospital Saturday', initiated in 1875 and taking place annually, first in November and later in July, for some years. In the 1880s the Hospital Saturday Committee organised fetes at Coxley Valley, then a favourite place of resort, with music, dancing, swings and coconut shies. There was also Hospital Sunday at the

Figure 20: Clayton Hospital and Wakefield Dispensary in Wood Street. *Yorkshire Archaeological Society*

Figure 21: Clayton Hospital. *The John Goodchild Collection*

end of November each year, founded by 1871, when the offertory from local churches and chapels was collected for the hospital.

At a public meeting here, just a year later, the Wakefield branch of the St John's Ambulance Association was formed with the specific aim of training policemen, railway workers, and mill workers in how to deal with people who had been injured in accidents. The advice was to 'send for the doctor and then hold on to the wounded life until he comes'. One of the first ambulances in the area, that of Sharlston Colliery, was on display for the meeting. Further substantial endowments for Clayton Hospital came in 1892 when Samuel Fozzard Harrison left £23,000 to it.

The House of Recovery, sometimes simply called the Fever Hospital, at the corner of Westgate Common and Lawefield Lane, opened in 1826 (Figure 22). It was founded by a group of women led by Mrs Sharp, wife of the Vicar of Wakefield, Mrs Peterson of Warren House and Mrs Heywood of Wentworth House. It had five rooms and could take as many as twelve patients at a time. It had one nurse who was both housekeeper and matron and who was paid seven shillings a week with her board and lodging, coals and candles and a house servant. The institution's finances depended on voluntary subscriptions, bequests, and the annual Wakefield Charity Ball which shared the proceeds with the Dispensary, or ad hoc events such as the Yeomanry Cavalry Ball in February

Figure 22: The House of Recovery. *The John Goodchild Collection*

1848. It was intended for poor people with infectious fevers living within Wakefield township or less than a mile from its boundary. People were received on presentation of a certificate from a medical practitioner. In its first year it catered for twenty-two patients. including people with typhus fever, 'the dropsies', rheumatism, and spinal disease. In its busiest, 1847, it had seventy-one patients. Visitors were allowed between 2pm and 3pm. Its 'ambulance' was a sedan chair kept on the premises. There was some concern in 1827 that a patient suffering from typhus fever had been carried to the House in one of the chairs used by the general public, possibly thus spreading the infection. It closed in 1853 when the Dispensary moved to Wood Street and was able to provide five beds.

There had been a serious outbreak of cholera at Gawthorpe in 1825 when twenty people died and where, it was claimed, the weaving community was not poor but was certainly dirty; there were no wells; the only drinking water came from ponds.

Cholera came again in 1831, having spread westwards across Europe. Its arrival in England, with cases in Sunderland, was reported in the Wakefield paper in November. Wakefield people must have realised that it would inevitably reach the town and that it had inadequate facilities and strategies to cope with an epidemic. The Constable was immediately requistioned to call a public meeting. Here it was resolved to establish an ad hoc Board of Health made up of magistrates, Anglican clergy and Nonconformist ministers, the parochial authorities, and two inhabitants from each of the three divisions of the town. The Board was authorised to take whatever measures were necessary to cleanse and purify the streets, the alleys, and the homes of the poor, and to negotiate for any building they thought desirable for a hospital. Money was to be raised by subscription. The meeting determined that any shortfall must come from the Poor Rate. A Wakefield surgeon, William Dawson, visited Sunderland to talk to the doctors there, visit the Poor House, and learn all he could of the treatment of the disease. Cholera first reached Wakefield in July 1832 breaking out at the House of Correction where there were 529 prisoners. Seventy-five of these who were nearing the end of their sentences were immediately released, perhaps a short-sighted measure as one of them carried the cholera to Hampole and another to Clayton Heights. The visiting magistrates ordered an improved diet, with more meat and good beer; vegetables and cheese were excluded. Dr Caleb Crowther provided an account of the treatment of the prisoners: they were placed in a warm bed and well rubbed with a hot flannel and turpentine; they were given ten grains of calomel and sixty drops of tincture of opium with warm brandy and water; some of the patients were bled from the arm. It was six weeks after the first cases at the prison before cholera appeared in Wakefield beyond the prison walls but between August and October there were some sixty-two deaths from the disease. The Overseers of the Poor opened a soup kitchen in Northgate and distributed 120 pairs of blankets and 1,400 yards of calico among people living primarily at Eastmoor and at Westgate Common.

There was a second serious cholera outbreak in the autumn of 1849. The Board of Guardians appointed an additional medical officer and did what it could to improve the sanitary state of the town under the Nuisance Removal and Diseases Prevention Act . The majority of cases were in Nelson Street and the surrounding yards where there was no drainage and the effluent from privies contributed to the stagnant green water on the street surface. At an inquest on two of the dead, a police officer reported finding thirty-six people crammed together in a two-room house.

An Eye Dispensary for the poor, evidently founded by churchmen, was in existence in Westgate, perhaps at the House of Recovery, by 1842. Funds included the occasional fine passed on from magistrates. In 1853 it was amalgamated with Wakefield Dispensary.

The Dispensary and the House of Recovery were for the sick but sane poor of Wakefield. But provision was urgently needed in the early nineteenth century for the poor with mental health problems not just in Wakefield but in the county as a whole. Following the County Asylums Act of 1808, the West Riding magistrates, in 1818 provided its Pauper Lunatic Asylum in the Stanley cum Wrenthorpe township on land to the west of Aberford Road (Figure 23). It was only the sixth to be built by magistrates in the country although there had been private asylums before this such as the Retreat, at York, established by William Tuke, a Quaker tea merchant, in 1796. The first block of the Wakefield asylum was H-shaped to allow for maximum supervision. The building was lit by gas obtained from whale oil. Its

Figure 23: The Pauper Lunatic Asylum. *Wakefield MDC Cultural Services*

Figure 24: The Theatre at Stanley Royd. *The author*

medical officers adopted the scientific understanding of the day in their approach and encouraged a humane ethos. Occupational therapy included work such as weaving, or winding bandages. There were occasional treats such as excursions to Walton Hall. The asylum had its own chaplain and chapel. James Crichton Browne, the medical director from 1866-1876, encouraged theatrical entertainment. A large detached hall was provided in 1859, initially as a dining and recreation room. This swiftly became, also, a ballroom and theatre (Figure 24). It was sometimes billed jocularly as the Theatre Royal, Stanley-cum-Wrenthorpe. W S Gilbert brought his play, 'Acis and Galatea' there in the spring of 1875. The building was extended in October 1893 with a new stage and, beneath it, dressing rooms.

Those sane poor who were unable to maintain themselves and could not be easily maintained by the Overseers in their own homes were housed in the workhouse. In 1800 the township workhouse was at the top of Thornhill Street (Figure 25). Henry Clarkson referred to it as 'Comprised within a very small area'. It was frequently condemned for its indiscriminate herding and its likelihood to deprave. For a time, following their inception in 1837, the Board of Guardians continued to rent the old workhouse although in 1849 they recognised that it was 'unhealthy, inconvenient, and too highly rented'. In 1851, when it held 103 people, *The Wakefield Journal* noted, 'In the females' day room there are several idiotic and also some insane girls and, as is frequently the case that girls of the town, full of loathsome disease, have to be sent into the house, there is no separate place to put them in and they are left to mix with the other inmates whom they contaminate by their obscene language and songs'. It is hard to determine whether economic or social factors proved the stronger impulse to persuade the Guardians to built a new workhouse. The Right Honourable J G Smyth argued, in line with the thinking behind the 1834 Poor Law Amendment Act, that a much larger building would actually save money because there would be less need to maintain paupers with 'out relief'. The district Poor Law inspector, H B Farnell, urged the Board not to be afraid of sending paupers to the new workhouse; it would be cheaper than supporting them at home and would be morally beneficial:

> *I am convinced that sending paupers to the workhouse is the most effectual plan for decreasing their number as those persons who have been used to an irregular mode of life do not like the regularity and restraint of the workhouse.*
>
> *They do not like getting up at a fixed hour in the morning to breakfast, being regularly washed in the baths at a particular time, and so on. This uniformity of conduct is so disagreeable for them that rather than submit to it many of the able-bodied paupers will turn out and work.*

Figure 25: The old workhouse as drawn by Henry Clarke. *Wakefield Historical Society*

Farnell urged the Guardians to provide a school for the children and remarked:

While you are doing what you can for the heads of the children you should harden their hands also and teach them the way to become labourers, making them happy and moral men and women

The new Workhouse, opened in November 1852 in Park Lodge Lane, had its own hospital. The complex was designed by J E Oates of York and was intended to house the elderly, the infirm and the destitute. It cost £8,000. The entrance building provided a board room, an office for the clerk, modest residential accommodation for the porter, and rooms for 'probationers'. At either end of this building were wards for vagrants who were segregated from the rest of the community. There were three parallel buildings about 100 feet apart. The main one, which was 210 feet long and three storeys high, held the 'regular' inmates in eight distinct categories; each 'class' had its own day-room, wash-room, dormitories, exercise court, water closets and staircases. The 'classes' had contact with each other only when they were taken to the dining-hall. The third building was the infirmary. This was 132 feet long and had separate wards for men, women, boys and girls, each with its bathroom, lavatories and nurses' room. On the first floor were wards for people with infectious diseases. At each end of the block was a single-storey building containing the 'idiot day rooms and dormitories'. Large cisterns on the roof provided hard and soft water, the latter from rain. This was intended for paupers but, in the absence of any other fever hospital, cases of small pox among non-paupers were treated there too, sometimes at the expense of Wakefield Corporation. After the election of the first women to the Board in 1894, and perhaps with some influence from them, the Guardians opened a splendid new infirmary in 1899 (Figure 26). There was, by then, a new emphasis nationally on professional nursing. The hospital was designed by William Watson to provide 150 beds and was one of the first buildings

Figure 26: The workhouse hospital. *The author's collection*

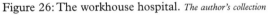

Figure 27: Dr Crowther's almshouses. *The John Goodchild Collection*

in Wakefield to be lit by electricity. Accommodation was in an E-shaped building. The two outer wings, or pavilions, provided separate wards for men and women.

Outside the workhouse, the poor were helped in various ways by the Overseers, primarily by out-relief, in terms of tickets for food or medicine.

The elderly poor who were fortunate enough to be provided with an almshouse avoided the workhouse. Almshouses have a long tradition, the earliest Wakefield ones dating from the late-sixteenth century. Almshouse Lane owes its name to those provided in 1647 by Cotton and William Horne. The philanthropic practice of endowing them re-emerged in the latter part of the nineteenth century and some of the almshouses remain in use in the twenty-first century. Divisions between the Established Church and Nonconformity had an effect on the provision: Caleb Crowther, who was physician to the Wakefield Dispensary, established a trust in 1838, buying land at the corner of George Street and Thornhill Street where the outer walls and roof of the future almshouses were erected. Under the terms of his will, the almshouses were completed and opened in 1863 (Figure 27). Because Crowther had been horrified at the conditions imposed by the Governors of the Wakefield Charities when they would admit only the Anglican orthodox to almshouses, he made it clear that neither his alms people nor trustees should be members of the Church of England. In 1887, one of the Crowther trustees, George E Smith, provided the charity with the funds for

a futher six almshouses in Westfield Road. Joseph Marsland (1819-1897), a
worsted spinner and colliery proprietor, built six cottages in Paddock Road,
Primrose Hill, and created a trust in 1886 providing these for the benefit of poor,
deserving women. His architect was Frederick Simpson. In 1890 he gave the trust
a further three houses and a mission room at the same site. Major Joseph Barker
(his commission was in the local Rifle Volunteers) endowed almshouses in
Holmefield Avenue, Thornes, in 1887. These came into the possession of the
Corporation in the 1890s. Old and dilapidated almshouses at Pledwick, then in
the care of the Overseers of the Poor of Sandal township, were bought in 1885 by
retired lawyer Samuel Fozzard Harrison and rebuilt to the design, again, of
Frederick Simpson. Harrison, who died in 1892, left £6,000 in his will for the
continued maintenance of the almshouses. There were many other charities. For
example, in 1825 Joseph Harrison left £5 each, twice a year, to twenty poor men
and women who were of good character and members of the Established Church.
His sister-in-law, Sarah Harrison provided in her will of 1858 for a further ten
poor men and women to receive a bible and a prayer book each and £5 every 24
June and 21 December.

Wakefield appointed its first Medical Officer of Health (on a part-time basis at
£30 a year) in 1866. He was William Swift Wade and remained in office until
1903. In 1873 his salary was raised from £30 to £50. He was also the police
surgeon and treated patients in the lock-up. The Corporation's first 'hospital'
came, under Wade's direction, in 1871 in the form of two tents for small-pox
patients in the corner of a field at Park Hills quite close to the Workhouse. One
tent was for the nurses and the other, measuring thirty by sixteen feet and divided
by a canvas partition, was for the patients. There was a serious fire in December
1871 when a gas heater set the canvas ablaze and a nurse and two patients died.
Perhaps it was this fire, the prevalence of small-pox and other highly infectious
diseases, and perhaps the cost of paying the Guardians to take some of their
townspeople, that led Wakefield City Council, in its capacity as the Local Board
of Health, to take its next steps in 1872 to provide in-patient treatment. The
council decided to build its own fever hospital on a site in Park Lodge Lane close
to the workhouse. So in 1874 Park Lodge Lane was levelled, sewered and flagged.
William Watson (amidst controversy) was commissioned to design the buildings
(Figure 28). A loan of £3,000 was negotiated from the Public Works Loan
Commission. Wakefield would pay 3.5% interest and the debt had to be repaid in
30 years. In 1893 the hospital took in 295 cases of small-pox.

Outside Wakefield, the Wakefield Rural Sanitary Authority built an infectious
diseases hospital at Carr Gate in 1889.

A convalescent home for women and children was opened in 1888 at Lupset
Lodge on Horbury Road, Lupset. The home was intended for people who were
convalescent, rather than ill, but who needed to rest and recuperate for a period
of two weeks or, in some cases, a month (Figure 29). The scheme had been
proposed in Queen Victoria's golden jubilee year and was promoted by Lady

Figure 28: The southern block of Wakefield Isolation Hospital, *c*1890. *Wakefield MDC Cultural Services*

Figure 29: Lupset Lodge. *The John Goodchild Collection*

Catherine Milnes Gaskell of Thornes House. The secretary was Ann Clarkson and the treasurer was (Miss) E E Fennell. It was dependent on annual subscriptions and gifts and the support of the specially-formed Guild of Pity. At the time of its first Annual Report, the Guild had 239 members and a further 101 associates. Wakefield City Tradesmen's Association supported the home with donations from its annual fetes, held in Clarence Park. It was regularly provided with fresh milk and vegetables from Thornes House. Mrs Simpson, wife of the soap manufacturer, gave quantities of soap. Mrs Lewis of Thornes Vicarage read to patients. Dr Wright gave his services free as did Dr Reader who had followed him by 1899. The matron received a salary of £23 15s a year. The food bill in the first year was £63. Patients were admitted on the recommendation of a subscriber who paid £1 1s a week for their maintenance. The home closed in 1915.

Wakefield's Medical Officer was able to report in 1900 that, certainly for the first time in the history of its Corporation, the death rate was lower than the national average.

On their discharge from prison, young women were provided for in the House of Refuge opened in 1842 in a house at the north-west corner of St John's Square. It was founded by Mrs Hamer, the widow of a Barnsley solicitor. For a time between 1854 and 1865, with grant-aid from the Government, it served also as a Reformatory. In 1866 day-to-day responsibility was undertaken by Charlotte Emily Armytage, wife of the Governor of Wakefield Prison, and the institution became the West Riding Industrial Home for Discharged Female Prisoners. She remained its superintendent until her death in May 1919. When a grand four-day bazaar was held in the Corn Exchange in 1870, in support of the Home, public-spirited people from towns throughout the West Riding provided stalls. The event was opened by Lord Houghton. Wholly new premises were built on the same site in 1872, providing a day-room cum classroom, dining room, and dormitory accommodation for up to forty young women. Designed by Swinden Barber of Halifax, it had a chapel on the second floor. A laundry enabled the residents to learn to wash and provided a source of income.

An Industrial Home for men was opened at the junction of Westgate and Back Lane in 1864, again for the benefit of those discharged from the prison. They were employed in making mats and matting.

The nineteenth century saw many other voluntary efforts to help the poor, especially in times of severe bad weather or economic depression. Public meetings, like that in the Moot Hall in January 1801, led to the forming of committees to raise subscriptions and distribute aid, often in the form of soup and bread. Prosperous individuals such as T Halliley of Chald House (1843) distributed such items as soap, coal and woollen petticoats among their poor neighbours.

From time to time ad hoc soup kitchens were set up by other bodies. In January 1875, during another period of economic depression, the Wakefield Licensed

Victuallers Association established a soup kitchen at the *Bull and Mouth Hotel*, placing an immediate order for 1,200 lbs of bread and 30 stones of meat. Later in 1875 Wakefield gained a permanent, and, in 1876, purpose built, Poor Invalid Kitchen. Soup and bread were served throughout the winter months to those who could afford little else and the kitchen's specialities were nourishing beef tea and milk puddings to be carried to the homes of the invalid poor. In the winter of 1886 it distributed 2,000 loaves and 50 gallons of soup a week. At the same time, the former hospital premises in Wood Street was opened on Sundays to provide free breakfasts. The Invalid Kitchen was an interdenominational and interparty charity, begun as a School of Cookery by the Wakefield branch of the Yorkshire Council of Education with a night school for elementary education for women and girls. The trustees appointed in 1875 included the Reverend C J Camidge (the vicar of Wakefield), the Reverend W M Madden (vicar of Holy Trinity) and the Reverend J S Eastmead, minister of Salem Independent Chapel in George Street together with the two political rivals, T K Sanderson (the Tory maltster who was Wakefield's member of Parliament at the time) and Robert B Mackie (his Liberal opponent). The School of Cookery was taken over by the Wakefield School Board by 1890 and was moved to 14 Howard Street. The kitchen survived until the end of the First World War.

Wakefield Clothing Society, established by 1843, helped the poor to help themselves by collecting deposits against the purchase of clothes and blankets. The deposits were supplemented by philanthropists' subscriptions.

Many working people helped themselves rather more effectively by joining one or other of the various Friendly Societies which flourished from the late eighteenth century, primarily, in Wakefield, the Odd Fellows. In 1837 there were ten lodges of Odd Fellows and one each of Druids, Foresters, Free Gardeners and Ancient Shepherds. Individual lodge names could be quite remarkable! In 1848 the Elephant Triumphant Lodge of the Grand United Order of Oddfellows held its meeting at the *Great Bull Hotel*. In 1839, when their rules were submitted to the West Riding Magistrates, the Friendly Society of Odd Women was meeting at the *Kirkgate Hotel*. Following the cholera outbreak of 1849, a special sermon was preached in December to raise funds for the Oddfellows whose resources had been much depleted by the expense of members' funerals. The (national) High Court of the Ancient Order of Foresters met for a week in the Music Saloon in 1850 with some 100 representatives attending from all over the country. The Foresters, who liked to dress up as characters from the Robin Hood legends, held a great procession in Wakefield in May 1852 and no doubt on many other occasions.

Friendly societies held *ad hoc* events for the poor or the aged: the Royal Antediluvian Order of Buffaloes began a tradition in 1892 of provided a knife and fork tea for old people in the Music Saloon at Christmas. By 1898 the numbers attending were so great that the event was held at the Corn Exchange.

The Borough Cemetery

One of the central recommendations in the Report of William Ranger, delivered in 1852, was that 'no time should be lost in the formation of a general cemetery, so that the existing burial grounds, particularly those connected with the parish church, may no longer be used as places of interment'. There were burial grounds associated with St Andrew's, St John's and St James's Churches, the Baptist, Congregational – both Salem and Zion – and Unitarian Chapels, the Friends' Meeting House and West Parade Chapel. But the parish church and its yard had been used for many centuries. Since records began in 1613, there had by 1852 been 47,625 interments in the grounds of the parish church, and a further 2,299 in the church itself. A part of the Vicarage Croft, lying between the Springs and the vicarage itself, was utilised as an overflow ground from 1811 and in 1815 was formally conveyed to trustees for this purpose. In a mere forty years it had seen 10,230 burials. (The residence of the Vicars of Wakefield, moved in 1877 to Carlton House, on the corner of Sandy Walk and Cliff Hill. It remained in use as the vicarage until 1919.)

A scheme was got up in 1849-50 to provide a new cemetery and some £500 was raised in subscriptions. The scheme seems to have been hi-jacked by the Established Church. Three sites were considered, one near Red Hall on the turnpike road to Leeds, a piece of ground belonging to the vicar of Wakefield in the Swadlingstones, and land at Thornes adjoining Thornes Churchyard. The last of the three schemes was preferred although it meant that burials would be the

Figure 30: The Borough Cemetery. *The author*

province of the incumbent of St James's Church rather than Wakefield parish church. However the scheme foundered.

Until 1857, the Corporation itself had no powers to establish a cemetery. Whilst the township could have done so, the adjoining townships of Alverthorpe with Thornes and Stanley cum Wrenthorpe, each of which lay partly in the borough, refused to co-operate since they felt little need of a new facility and demurred at the cost. Once Wakefield gained powers, by an Order in Council of February 1857 to provide a borough cemetery, it promptly bought the estate at Belle Vue from Sir Lionel Pilkington for £5,000. Twin chapels – one for the Established Church and the other for Nonconformists – were designed by M O Tarbotton, the borough surveyor. William Barratt, the nurseryman whose grounds were in the St John's area, planted trees and shrubs. The first burial was on 13 April 1859 a few weeks before the burial ground was consecrated on 18 June, by the Bishop of Ripon (Figure 30). By a further Order in Council later the same year the Vicarage Croft was closed for burials as were the burial grounds at St Andrew's, the Baptist, Zion and Salem chapels, and the old Friends' burial ground.

The water supply

The sole sources of water in Wakefield until 1837 were springs, wells, streams, becks, and rainwater. The better houses had their own wells or pumps, often referred to in advertisements for their letting or sale, e.g. 'a capital messuage in an elevated and airy part of the town with a pump having an excellent supply of water'. But there were public wells, too. John Hewitt, who published *The History and Topography of Wakefield* in 1862 referred to the wells in the Springs, and to Jacob's Well, and Ings Well at Primrose Hill. Dr Walker, quoting an account of the Ancient Wells of Wakefield, written in 1822, notes that there were Pincheon Well (in the upper part of Pincheon Street), Ing Well (in Ingwell Croft), Norton Well (in Norton Croft, later to become Gas House Yard), Rectory Well in the grounds of the Rectory but used by neighbours, Vicarage Well (in Vicarage Lane where there was a second, unnamed, well), Windy Well (to the east of St John's), Park Well (on the top of the hill near Park Lodge), Toad-Hole Well (at the bottom of Park Hills), and Westbury Well (again at Park Hills). St Swithin's Well, not far from Clarke Hall, had in the eighteenth century a bath house and bath, for people to experience the supposedly curative waters. There was also a spa and small bath-house, recalled in the name New Wells, in Thornhill Street which had gained some fame in the 18 century again because of its supposed healing powers. Before the Water Company was established, water carriers sometimes passed through the streets retailing water they had drawn from the wells.

In 1837 a joint-stock company was formed, authorised by Act of Parliament to take water from the River Calder at Stanley Ferry. It was unable to take purer water from a higher reach of the Calder because of the rights of the Wakefield Soke Mills. The water was pumped by a steam engine to a six-acre reservoir off Ouchthorpe Lane, Stanley. This brought water into the town but its condition was unsavoury. 'Not infrequently living or dead objects issue from the pipes', it was observed. The local authority's practice, from 1862, of pouring all the sewage from Wakefield into the Calder just two miles above the company's pump, added to the fouled nature of the supply. The company provided water simply on an economic basis: 'The question was not whether a street or district was in want of water but whether the revenue derived will pay for the cost of outlay.' In 1842, when the Wakefield Humanity Society called for subscriptions to provide pipes and water troughs there, no water was available for the hundreds of animals at the Cattle Market. In 1849 there was a complaint that the water at Jacob's Well, once the best in town, had become 'befouled with waste from a coal-pit stream' which was 'a great loss to poor people who cannot afford to take the Waterworks Company water'. By 1852, 2,655 homes were supplied with water. Elsewhere people fetched it from service cocks. But the water was impure and the flow was unpredictable. In January 1866, for example, the company installed two new boilers and a new 55hp pumping engine (called Sarah!) in a specially-built engine house to try to maintain a constant supply. At the same time, Wakefield councillors resolved that it was 'of the opinion that the present water supply to the inhabitants of the borough as well as many other towns in the West Riding is in many instances very deficient in quantity and in all cases inferior in quality being impregnated with the town's sewage as well as mineral and other impurities and is therefore unfit for domestic or even manufacturing purposes.' The company tried to improve the quality of the water by filtration, first using cocoa-nut fibre, then sand, and from 1864, carbide of iron.

A printed leaflet of 1867 shows the charges made by the Company for water for domestic and for industrial use. An additional 8s a year was charged for private houses with baths, with another 6s a year for any water closets. Cottage dwellings were to pay only 3s a year for water closets and where a group of cottages shared a closet the annual charge was 2s.

Almost from its incorporation, some members of Wakefield Council had aimed to acquire the Water Company, most notably Henry Lee. There were abortive negotiations in 1853-4 but the problem was always one of cost.

From 1871, the Waterworks Company promoted a series of schemes to provide a new and pure source of water. It twice promoted bills for pumping water from the ground at Park Hills, planning to provide water for Altofts, Newland, Normanton, Warmfield, Snydale and Sharlston. The Corporation objected on the grounds that the water would be too hard and that the Wakefield ratepayers would be subsidising people elsewhere. The Company was still taking its water from the by-now heavily polluted Calder in 1873, when a further offer from the Corporation to buy it was rejected and it secured an Act for building a further reservoir at Field Head. There was an urgent need for an adequate supply of fresh water and as a consequence of the rejection, a rival Wakefield concern, the New Waterworks Company, was promptly founded, with Henry Lee as Chairman of the Directors, and in August 1873, to the disquiet of the people of Penistone, was

Figure 31: Ardsley Reservoir. *The author*

prospecting for water in its parish. The emergence of a rival, prompted the old company to devise a new scheme. Early in 1874, both companies announced their intention to promote bills in Parliament, each of them involving a new reservoir, taking water from the Lower Don, at Langsett. Wakefield Council, holding a special and fraught meeting, determined to support the bill of the original company and to oppose that of the new one. The ostensible reason was that the old company already had its mains in place in the town whilst the scheme of the new company would involve a good deal of disruption to the streets. Faced with this situation, the shareholders of the new company agreed, for £5,500 compensation, to withdraw their bill. The original company's bill was defeated in Parliament because of opposition from landowners in the area it would have affected and from Sheffield Corporation. Another scheme in the autumn of 1874 was to buy surplus water from the Holmfirth Reservoir Company.

In 1875 the quality of Wakefield's water was improved when Robert Hudson and Co. sank for coal close to Field Head, and fed the water from their shaft into the water company's reservoir. The company then sank for water in the same area. A third of the water supply then came from this shaft.

There was yet another Waterworks Company bill: in 1876 a scheme was put before Parliament, which involved pumping water from underground near

Darfield where four million gallons of water a day was being pumped from Wath Main Colliery. Wakefield Corporation opposed this at the select-committee stage on the grounds that the water would be far too hard. Henry Lee, himself a councillor, opposed the scheme avowedly on behalf of his family's textile concern, George Lee and Sons, which required soft water. In May the Council proposed taking its opposition to the House of Lords. The following month agreement was at last reached with the Water Company for its purchase. Without further opposition the Waterworks Company's Act gained royal assent in August, authorising the building of reservoirs at Houghton Magna and Chevet. It was never implemented. The Council's own, immensely ambitious, Improvement Act of 1877 empowered it both to build its Town Hall (at last) and to buy the Waterworks Company, the latter at a cost of £210,000 with all debts to be cleared in 70 years. A Waterworks Committee was established in July 1877. In 1879 the Council provided new filter beds at the Stanley reservoir and installed a new pumping engine at Stanley Ferry. These were, however, only temporary measures. By July 1879 the Council was planning a further parliamentary bill to authorise its taking water from the Rishworth moors near Ripponden. In February 1880 they reached agreement with the owners of Crumlin Mill at Rishworth to protect their water rights. The Act, passed in July 1880, giving Wakefield the necessary powers, provided for the construction of Green Withens, Ringstone and Ardsley Reservoirs, filter beds at Kirkhamgate and a small reservoir at Lindle Hill to provide water to the Pauper Lunatic Asylum (Figure 31). Water was turned into the holding reservoir at Ardsley in October 1887 and the supply to Wakefield was turned on, amid considerable rejoicing and junketing, on 1 May 1888. A procession of carriages, waggonettes and charabancs went first to Ardsley to let the water down to the city, returning to the Town Hall, where a temporary fountain had been set up, for the Mayor, Alderman Henry Lee, to turn it on there. The first sod of a second Rishworth reservoir, Green Withens, was cut on 23 June 1892. But even at the end of the century poorer districts were without adequate water.

Lighting

Until 1823 the principal streets of Wakefield were lit by whale-oil lamps provided by the Street Commissioners. In 1801, one man was employed to light them all for the hours of darkness for all but six nights a month; the three days before the full moon, the day of the full moon itself, and the two days after the full moon were regarded as light enough already. From 1802 to 1806 the Commissioners gave annual contracts for looking after the lamps to a London entrepreneur, William Couldery. (He had been engaged by the Lichfield Conduit Lands Trustees to light their lamps in 1798-99.) But his employees proved unsatisfactory and they went back to their own earlier lamplighter, Joseph Morton, in the autumn of 1806.

However, following a public meeting in the Court House on 6 October 1821, chaired by the Vicar of Wakefield, the Reverend Samuel Sharp, an Act of Parliament was obtained to establish the Wakefield Gaslight Company. An acre of land at Oliver Ings, to the north of Warrengate, was acquired and the designs of the engineer, John Malam, were swiftly implemented. The foundation stone of the gas works was laid on 18 September 1822. The Street Commissioners negotiated with the Company for the provision of gas lighting and the first 104 gas lamps were lit at the end of January 1823. Gas was available for shops, factories and mills. The works were extended in 1846 (Figure 32). The House of Correction had its own gas works.

Whilst by the end of the century, Wakefield Corporation had acquired the Waterworks Company, the Gas Company prospered independently until it was bought out in 1943 by the United Kingdom Gas Corporation which, in turn was nationalised in 1949.

Wakefield Corporation built its own electricity generating station in the 1890s. An Electric Lighting Committee was set up in November 1893 to secure the necessary order from Parliament (obtained in 1894) and to oversee arrangements for borrowing capital (£25,000), securing a consulting engineer, commissioning designs for the plant and implementing them.

Since Wakefield required a sewage works at much the same time as it embarked on its electricity project, a site was purchased on Calder Vale Road, just to the north-east of the railway line, for both schemes.

The sole purpose of the power station, initially, was to provide electricity for

Figure 32: The offices of the Wakefield Gas Company. *The author*

lighting, especially street lighting, although in 1895 the Committee had its first enquiry about power for tramways. As the project developed approaches were made to the Committee about lighting some of Wakefield's major institutions: an early request came in 1894 from the churchwardens at Wakefield Cathedral; in 1895 the School Board asked about the cost of providing electricity to its new school in Ings Road; in 1896 the Guardians of the Wakefield Poor Law Union raised the question with the Committee of providing electricity for the new workhouse infirmary and there were discussions too in regard to the projected County Hall in Wood Street. In January 1897 the Trustees of the Methodist West Parade Chapel inquired about electricity and in September that year the County Council was in touch about a new building at the Pauper Lunatic Asylum.

Power was switched on on Saturday, 13 November, 1897. It had not come without controversy. The Committee had elected to build an underground substation at the top of Westgate and, whilst digging a large hole, the Council decided to kill two birds with one stone and to erect a men's lavatory down there as well. City residents objected and the London Midland Bank, with its premises facing the hole, threatened to sue for damages to its property. But the success of the electricity undertaking was manifest when County Hall, which was completed in 1898, was wired for electricity from the outset. The period light switches, in an art nouveau style, remain fascinating and, with their curvaceous naked women somewhat erotic, features.

The Post Office
Wakefield had had postmasters since the mid-seventeenth century. The first Royal Mail coach from London to York, taking in Sheffield, Barnsley and Wakefield, ran in 1786. From 1829 a gig ran daily between Wakefield and Huddersfield to carry the mail swiftly. Pressure from Wakefield people led the Postmaster General in 1838 to take steps to ensure that mail from London reached Wakefield by 4pm rather than at some time between 7 and 10pm. For much of the nineteenth century, its main – and for some decades the only – post office moved from place to place depending on what building the local postmaster provided. In 1809 the post office moved from Old Green Yard to the corner of Cross Street and Wood Street. From there it moved to Silver Street (1813), Radcliffe Place (1817), the top of Westgate (1833), Wood Street (1863), and the rear of the Bull Hotel (1873). From 1868 Wakefield Chamber of Commerce pressed the Postmaster General to establish a Crown Post Office in the town. In 1876 their wish was granted. But there was strong opposition, from the Chamber of Commerce and Wakefield Corporation, and less wholeheartedly from the Chamber of Trade, to the chosen site in Market Street, then belonging to John Tuling Sweeting of the *Great Bull Hotel*. The Chamber of Commerce called a public meeting in the then Town Hall in Crown Court. The preference was for a site at the top of Westgate, to the east of Queen Street opposite the Church Institute. Close to the great Corn Exchange, the site would have demanded a costly, handsome building. The site

Figure 33: The Post Office in Market Street. *The Wakefield Express*

was available for £3,800 where the Market Street site, with an eighty foot street frontage, would cost only £2,000. There were calls for subscribers to make up the difference. Insufficient funds were raised and the modest Market Street building was opened on 1 August 1876 (Figure 33). It remained in use until 1981 when the new premises in Denby Dale Road were opened. The first post box in Wakefield, in Wood Street, was erected in 1809. There were further letter boxes in 1856 at the junction of Wentworth Terrace and Bond Street, at the fork of the roads to Horbury and Dewsbury on Westgate Common, and at the junction of Warrengate and Pincheon Street. In 1876 there were, additionally, boxes for the collection of letters in Kirkgate, George Street, Wentworth Street, Westgate Common, Warrengate, and at Kirkgate and Westgate Stations. In 1893 letter boxes were placed in Wakefield omnibuses. A pillar box was sited at the corner of Charlotte Street and Kirkgate in 1895.

Wakefield's first sub-post office came in 1841 at the bottom of Kirkgate. A sub post office was established at Sandal in 1848. By the 1880s there were sub postoffices at Thornes Road, Agbrigg, Newmillerdam, Eastmoor, Belle Vue, St John's and New Scarborough. These were run normally in conjunction with another business: for example Arthur Higgins, who ran the Eastmoor Post Office in 1892, was a grocer. Hewell and Son at Thornes Lane post office were house furnishers.

Wakefield led the way in bringing about the founding in 1897 of the National Federation of Sub Postmasters. Their work had grown with the introduction of the Post Office Savings Bank in 1861, the taking over of the telegraph system (which had reached Wakefield in 1852) in 1870 and the introduction of postal orders in 1872. The parcel post, which required the provision of weighing scales, began in 1883. Sub postmasters provided their premises, were given no paid holidays and no cover for illness. They also had to pay for the erection of their telegraph poles. Two local postmasters, Joseph Ranns and John Cussons, convened a meeting in the Music Saloon in Wood Street in 1897 and the National Association was formed.

Local Newspapers

At the beginning of the nineteenth century, Wakefield people depended on *The Leeds Mercury* which had been founded in 1718, or *The York Courant*, first published in 1725, *The Leeds Intelligencer* and its 1866 successor *The Yorkshire Post* to place advertisements and for (a modicum of) local news. But from 1804, Wakefield has been without its own local weekly newspaper for a little less than a year. In some periods, political rivalry between the Tories and the Liberals/Radicals was so strong that each had its own organ. *The Wakefield Star and West Riding Advertiser*, first issued in 1803 and published by a Mr Arnold from the 'Music Hall', foundered very briefly but was revived within weeks in May 1804 when it was taken over by Rowland Hurst. It was then edited by the liberal-minded clergyman Martin Naylor (1764-1843). In March 1811, when Hurst bought *The Halifax Journal* from J and B K Myers, and amalgamated the two papers, the new name *The Wakefield and Halifax Journal and Yorkshire and Lancashire Advertiser* was used. In the 1820s the paper carried very little local news and was largely made up of items taken from national or other regional papers, together with miscellaneous 'news' from many parts of the world. Naylor campaigned, however, as early as 1822, for the Yorkshire Assizes to be split up and for the West Riding business to come to Wakefield. He campaigned, too, for Parliamentary Reform. Inherited by

Rowland Hurst junior in 1830, the name of the paper was reduced to the simpler *Wakefield and Halifax Journal*. In 1833 Hurst sold the paper to Thomas Nichols. At this time, if not earlier Naylor relinquished the editorship. Nichols became bankrupt in 1834. The last issue of the paper came out on 13 May 1834. A new, and staunchly Tory paper, *The West Riding Herald and Wakefield Commercial and Agricultural Journal*, was first issued on 1 May 1835. Two years later, with the issue of 4 May 1837, it changed its name to *The Wakefield Journal and West Riding Herald* and adopted an impressive masthead with an engraving of the Corn Exchange. For a time it was edited by James Dibdin Hubbarde. It was bought by William Hepworth and Thomas Micklethwaite in October 1842 . Because Wakefield's corn market was 'one of the most important in the United Kingdom,' a second edition was produced on Friday afternoons to convey information about the trade to 'almost every newsroom in the kingdom'. The paper survived, albeit with several further name changes, until 1913.

Wakefield was without a Liberal voice from 1834 until the founding of *The Wakefield and West Riding Examiner*. The first issue, on 6 January 1849, announced that it was 'designed to supply a manifest want by representing and advocating the political, economical and social views of the general Liberal party in the Borough of Wakefield and the neighbouring towns'. Its concerns were to include

perfect Freedom of Trade, Economy and Retrenchment in General, Reduction of naval and military establishments, the extension of the suffrage at such times and by such means as the spread of education and intelligence among the unrepresented classes shall render expedient, the advancement of civil and religious liberty, and the total abolition of church rates.

In 1852 the liberal voice was stifled, briefly this time, when Thomas Micklethwaite (1813-1857) the Tory owner of *The Wakefield Journal and West Riding Herald* bought out the *Examiner. The Wakefield Journal and West Riding Herald* then became *The Wakefield Journal and Examiner and the West Riding Herald*.

With a parliamentary election pending, Wakefield Liberals needed to reassert their cause. A committee of leading Liberal townsmen persuaded John Robinson (1818-1879), who had a business in Southgate as a printer and bookseller, to found *The Wakefield Express*. It was, and has remained, a success, taking larger premises in Southgate soon after its inception. As stamp duty was abolished, in 1855, and as its sales increased, its cover price came down from 4.5d to 2d in 1860, and to 1d (when it was in competition with *The Wakefield Free Press*) The Robinson family continued to own the paper until the latter part of the twentieth century. The company became the Yorkshire Weekly Newspaper Group in 1979 and was purchased by the Johnston Press in 1985.

The rivalry between *The Express* and *The Journal* was personal as well as political. Micklethwaite referred to John Robinson as a 'snivelling and wretched nincompoop' and a 'fawnish, slavish hireling' whilst Robinson pointed out that Micklethwaite was a hypocrite in advocating temperance when he had been arrested for being drunk and disorderly in Barstow Square.

A further rival came on 1 November 1860 when William Rowlandson Hall published *The Wakefield Free Press*, free supposedly of political bias (its two rivals were, its editor claimed, conducted on 'obsolete and sectarian principles') although it was Liberal in tone and enjoyed Tory patronage. It aimed to recruit working-class readers with a cover price of 1d where the other two papers charged 3d. It also claimed to be the one truly local paper, eschewing filling its pages with re-cycled news from Barnsley, Dewsbury and Pontefract. The editorial in its first issue advocated more Parliamentary reform, noting that, almost thirty years after the great Reform Act, 'the people are still practically unrepresented in the house said to be theirs'. The working class as a body was, it claimed, 'sober, honest and intelligent'. Its editor and some, at least, of its contributors were Nonconformists and other of Hall's editorials attacked the vogue for ritualism in parts of the Anglican church and the imposition of the Church rate. In 1867, there was a series of lectures in Wakefield on the relationship between Church and State. (Hall, of course, was an advocate of disestablishment). The then Mayor, barrister William Shaw, in chairing one of these events, showed, in Hall's view (though he was apparently not alone) a very clear bias towards the Anglican speaker. Hall published a placard advertising the next issue of the paper and condemning the Mayor. The libel action which followed went as far as the West Riding Assizes in Leeds although the judge there instructed the jury to bring a verdict of 'not guilty'.

Hall brought out a daily evening paper, *The Free Press Evening News* from c1878 to c1883. *The Evening Press (Wakefield)* was started c1882 and ran until c1885. The British Library, which holds copies of some of these evening papers, also has issues of *Wakefield Saturday Night* from 1889 to 1891.

The Wakefield Echo, owner by Walter Carr and John Whiteley, was first published on 25 October 1876. It was initially issued fortnightly free of charge, depending on advertising revenue rather than on sales. In its first issue it asked when Wakefield could hope to have a public park and a museum. Later it came out weekly and was priced at 1d. It survived only until 1906.

For a time, between 1876 and 1900 Wakefield had four regular newspapers.

But where did people read not only the local papers but the regional and national ones? There was a news-room at the *White Hart* prior to 1809. A subscription newsroom was founded on 16 January 1809 at a meeting in the Crown Court Assembly Rooms. For a guinea a year members of the Newsroom could read a number of national and regional papers there. It was probably the same organisation for which the Wood Street Public Buildings were in part intended. At the annual meeting of subscribers on 1 May 1822 it was determined to negotiate with the proprietors of the Public Rooms to relocate there and to take *The Morning Chronicle, The Courier, The Traveller, The Times* (old and new), *The Globe, The Observer, the Leeds Intelligencer, The Leeds Mercury, The York Herald, the Hull Packet* and the *Wakefield and Halifax Journal*.

Rowland Hurst, the printer and newspaper publisher, established a subscription newsroom in 1815 in premises in Northgate. There were other ad hoc, and possibly shortlived, news and reading rooms. Wakefield Conservative Association established a newsroom, intended for general use, at the *White Hart Inn* in January 1837. A few weeks later Wakefield Temperance Society opened a newsroom at the newly opened *Temperance Hotel* in Westgate for subscribers paying 10s 6d a year. A newspaper advertisement in 1858 referred to the Mechanics' Institution newsrooms in Silver Street and Kirkgate which were open on weekdays from 7 or 8am until 10pm.

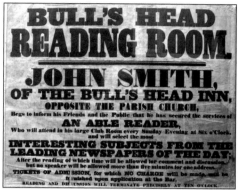

Reading rooms, where extracts from the newspapers were read aloud, and then perhaps discussed, were primarily for the illiterate. A surviving poster for the *Bull's Head*, probably of the 1840s, advertised the engagement of an 'able reader' (Figure 34).

Figure 34: A poster advertising the services of a reader at the *Bull's Head*. *The John Goodchild Collection*

The Fire Service

In the first half of the century, the township Constable was responsible for maintaining the town's fire equipment. There had been fire buckets stored above Westgate bar as early as the sixteenth century and there had been a fire engine by 1745. A new engine, first used in 1778, was housed in the base of the tower of the parish church. A further engine had been bought in 1793. In 1806 an engine was bought from the great engineer and inventor Joseph Bramah (1749-1814) who had patented a machine the previous year. A site was bought for this engine in New Street. In 1829 it was moved to King Street where, subsequently, all the township, and later the borough, fire engines were housed.

There were no official firemen in the first years of the century but those who worked at the pumps during a fire were paid by the Constable. At least one individual business had its own fire engine: in 1807 there was a major fire at the dressing shops of Steers and Allott. The engine from Holdsworth's Dyeworks was brought to the scene and assistance was given by members of the 51st Regiment then stationed in the town. The Royal Wakefield Volunteers 'preserved order'. Holdsworth's engine assisted, with those of the town and of the Leeds and Yorkshire Insurance Company when there was a fire at the Old Soke Mill at Wakefield Bridge in July 1838 (due to the friction of a corn screed).

The aftermath of an incident in New Street in 1836 provides an insight into how fire could be tackled at that time. Three engines were quickly on the scene. The conflagration, at the premises of a chemist and druggist, began in the upper floor and might have been caused by lightning. Mr Illingworth (perhaps he who had been deputy constable) attended with the Wakefield Town Engine No 2, ladders were put up against the building and a 'plentiful' supply of water was pumped into it. Second on the scene was the engine of the Leeds and Yorkshire County Insurance Company, under the direction of T H Wild, and finally another of the Town's engines arrived. Vast numbers of men were employed: each of the town's engines was manned by sixteen firemen; 121 other men were required to bring water or to man the pump. Wild brought sixty-two men.

The 1837 Act which established the Wakefield Waterworks Company made specific provision for the free use of the water supply in the event of a fire. In December 1849 the Council advertised the sale of two fire engines which were 'rendered unnecessary by the introduction of standards applied to Wakefield Waterworks' mains'.

At the time the new workhouse was under construction in 1852 there was a serious fire in its dining room. The Chief Constable. McDonnold, directed the efforts to put out the blaze. Both the town's engine and that of the Leeds and Yorkshire Insurance Company attended. The two engines were brought out again in September of the same year when there was a fire at the recently built worsted-spinning mill at Westgate Common (belonging then to Henry Clarkson) occupied by Messrs Thompson and Walker. The borough police manned the borough engine.

In 1858 the Leeds and Yorkshire Company withdrew its engine from Wakefield. The town bought a new engine with financial help from all the major insurance companies. However, on its first outing, in August, to attend a fire at Teall's grease works in Westgate, it proved entirely useless as the firemen did not know how to attach the hose! The fire-brigade chief resigned. The Chief Constable remained responsible for the fire service until the early years of the twentieth century.

Although Wakefield gained much in regard to amenities in the nineteenth century, the Corporation resisted all demands for a public library. There were, of course, subscription libraries and ones provided by the Church and Mechanics Institutes. There were calls in 1893, in particular from the Wakefield Working Men's Technical Association, for Wakefield council to adopt the Free Library Act, but it was not until 1906 that the city got a library 'on the rates'.

Sources

Caleb Crowther, unpublished account of the cholera epidemic of 1832 in the John Goodchild Collection
William Ranger, Report to the General Board of Health on a preliminary inquiry into the sewerage, drainage and supply of water, and the sanitary condition of the inhabitants of the borough of Wakefield, 1852.
John Todd and Lawrence Ashworth, The House: Wakefield Asylum 1818...1994
John Hewitt, The History and Topography of the Parish of Wakefield and its Environs, Wakefield (1862)
R S Duncan, Here we go Round the Mulberry Bush, 1994
Lupset Convalescent Home, Annual Reports, Wakefield Library Local Studies Dept. Box 8
Lichfield Public Services, A History of the County of Stafford; Volume 14: Lichfield, 1990.
K O M Golisti, 'Wakefield by Gaslight', in Aspects of Wakefield 2, 1999.
Eric Buckley, Wakefield Postal History, 1971.
Clayton, Brian, Wakefield's Postal History: Service through the Centuries, 1981
John Goodchild, 'The Constables and Town Officials of Wakefield', Wakefield Historical Society Journal, Vol 13, 2004

COMMUNICATIONS, TRADE AND INDUSTRY

Wakefield had already developed long before the nineteenth century as a retail market and as a major marketing centre for the textile industry, for both raw wool and finished cloth. John Leland remarked in the 1530s that the town's economy was based on coarse cloth. To the west of the town up the Calder valley, lay both moorland, suitable for grazing sheep rather than for agriculture, and a home-based cloth-making industry where the poor soils made agriculture on its own insufficient to maintain its people. The Pennine rivers and streams could power water mills. Mills for cloth fulling had been established on the River Calder in Wakefield itself in medieval times. Close to Wakefield itself, there were handloom weavers in Alverthorpe, Horbury, Ossett and Thornes. Until the coming of the railways in 1840, Wakefield was the principal wool stapling town in the West Riding. Wool was sent from all parts of England to the Wakefield staplers and then dispersed to the surrounding districts. Prosperous Wakefield cloth merchants had 'costly and elegant houses' including Georgian mansions in Westgate. By the sixteenth century Wakefield was trading in finished cloth. The Tammy Hall, where types of cloth known as Tammies and Camlets, were sold, had been built on a site between the present-day King Street and Wood Street, and opened on 10 July 1778. There were some 200 stalls, in the two-storey building. The cloth and wool-stapling trades declined in the first half of the nineteenth century, with the bulk of the white-cloth trade moving to Huddersfield and Leeds. Writing in 1854, George Tyas commented:

> The Wakefield of modern times is a quiet town, that has allowed its neighbours to outstrip it in size, population and industry. From its situation and local advantages, it should have become the metropolis of the West Riding; but when the manufacturing interest began to grow so amazingly in this country, it was not welcomed by the inhabitants of Wakefield, and so it settled down in Leeds and Bradford and other places. Wakefield thus lost an opportunity of improvement and progress which can never be recovered. At present it is important, not for its manufactures, but for its corn market and cattle fairs.

An editorial in *The Wakefield Journal and West Riding Herald* in 1850 remarked on the mansions in Westgate, once the abode of leading merchants, being divided and sub-divided, or tenantless, and of the capital expended on warehouses in Wakefield's yards which were by then standing empty.

However, as the century progressed, more diverse industries developed. The lost trades were replaced by the growth of worsted spinning, producing yarn for both hand-knitting and carpet manufacture. A somewhat partisan account of Wakefield in 1864 described it as 'inhabited by a pushing business people long trained in the urges of commerce and conspicuous by a superior intelligence as by an unwearied and persevering industry'.

Bricks had been made at Eastmoor for some time before 1709 when the Wakefield Manor Book recorded the current payment to the Lord of the Manor of 4d per 1,000 bricks. The industry continued there throughout the nineteenth century. Other brickyards developed to the north-west of Wakefield between the Dewsbury and Batley Roads. Henry Clarkson refers to Pemberton Milnes, whose Georgian town house of c1752 still stands in Westgate, always using his own bricks and having his kilns 'on the Ossett road, a short distance before the toll bar'.

Both coal mining and market gardening expanded in the mid nineteenth century, not infrequently making use of Irish labour. The only significant immigration in the nineteenth century was, in fact, of the Irish. Irishmen from the Leitrim area had come to Wakefield for temporary employment from the early years of the nineteenth century. Not surprisingly those who came to live in Wakefield permanently came from the same area. The immigration peaked in 1848-51. Initially they settled in Nelson Street, thence colonising New Street, Providence Street, Smallpage Yard and other nearby yards. In 1849, J H Charnock noted that 'Wakefield had market gardens from which many of the more densely populated towns of the West Riding were supplied.' Barratts, in the St John's area, was the largest of these. By at least 1822 they were, among much else, growing rhubarb, which, especially from the 1870s or 1880s when it was forced in heated sheds, was produced in market gardens in areas of Alverthorpe, Stanley and Thornes.

Whilst Wakefield's development in the nineteenth century was in the commercial and service sectors as well as in manufacturing, trade in coal, corn, malt, cattle and worsted yarns were all substantial elements of the economy. At the end of the century Wakefield was still one of the largest malt-producing centres in England.

The waterways

Wakefield was well placed for travel by road and water. The navigable waterways which had been developed in the eighteenth century were a major contributing factor to its trade. The River Calder had been made navigable to Wakefield by the Aire and Calder Navigation by about 1702. From 1826, Wakefield had access by water, via the new route of the Navigation to the new port of Goole which developed from that time. In 1838, *The Wakefield Journal* noted that fly boats could reach Goole in about eight hours and goods could be shipped from there to foreign ports. In 1839 the 'new cut', saving further time in travel, was opened

Figure 35: The aqueduct at Stanley Ferry. *The author*

from Broadreach to Fairies Hill across the pioneering aqueduct at Stanley Ferry (Figure 35). The Calder and Hebble Navigation, opened throughout in 1770, ran from its junction with the Aire and Calder for twenty-one miles from Wakefield to Sowerby Bridge. It connected with Sir John Ramsden's Canal at Cooper Bridge, and with the Rochdale Canal at Sowerby Bridge, enabling trade, in particular in corn and malt, with industrial Lancashire. The Barnsley Canal, opened from the Aire and Calder Navigation in 1799, was especially important for the transport of coal (Figure 36).

Figure 36: Coal barges passing on the Barnsley Canal. *The John Goodchild Collection*

Figure 37: Boat building on the Calder. *Wakefield Art Gallery*

With waterway connections to both agricultural areas to the east, and the industrial towns to the west, as well as to Barnsley, Wakefield had already begun to develop in the eighteenth century as an important inland port in particular for corn, but also for stone, timber, dyestuff, flax, and iron. Boat-building was begun at least by 1802. At Bottomboat, in the township of Stanley cum Wrenthorpe, Abraham Collinson, described as both a boat-builder and chapman or merchant, built sloops until he became bankrupt in 1817. John Collinson established a boat-building concern in Wakefield in 1822 which survived until 1841, when its then proprietor, Thomas Collinson, became bankrupt, and James Craven began boat-building in 1825 (Figure 37). The first boat to enter the new cut, in 1839, drawn by three grey horses and with outriders, was the 160 ton schooner, The James, built for Harrison and Co by Cravens. The firm was sold to Robert Stead in 1856. Just outside Wakefield, Samuel Womack began boat-building at Agbrigg in 1838. Warehouses and maltings, as well as mills, developed along the waterfront.

When the Canal Boats Act was passed in 1885, thirty-four working canal boats were registered in the Wakefield School Board area but with few families actually living on them.

The roads

Wakefield lay at the junction of major north-south routes and a road running up the Calder valley to the west. Under eighteenth century turnpike acts, the roads from Wakefield to Bradford, Doncaster, Horbury, Leeds and Sheffield had all been improved. An Act of Parliament of 1789 provided for a greatly improved road to York with the Wakefield to Aberford section running primarily across virgin land. An Act of 1825 provided for a completely new turnpike road to Denby Dale. The Calder was spanned by a suspension bridge. (One of the chains broke on 2 January 1836 plunging a waggon, a cart, and a gig into the water, and only timber props kept the bridge in use until the turnpike trust came to an end in 1874 and responsibility passed to the West Riding magistrates. The magistrates provided a new bridge in 1876, designed by their surveyor, Bernard Hartley.) Under an Act of 1831 a second, short and far less successful, new turnpike road was created across the Wakefield Ings from Kirkgate to Westgate. It was assumed that, despite the cost of the tolls, the new road would be viable because it shortened journeys from the south to the west. In fact people preferred the longer route via Kirkgate and Westgate to paying the tolls. The road was disturnpiked in 1863 and bought by Wakefield Corporation. The 1878 Highways and Locomotions Act gave responsibility for most main roads to the county magistrates. Most remaining turnpike trusts nationally were dissolved in the 1870s and 1880s and the Local Government Act of 1888 gave the responsibility for highways to the new County Councils.

There had been a regular mail coach from 1786 between London and Leeds passing through Wakefield. There were coaches in 1801 to Leeds and from there to Edinburgh, Leicester, Newcastle, Northampton, Nottingham, and London. A coach service from Wakefield to London, in the Lord Nelson, began in 1811, running on Mondays, Wednesdays and Fridays, leaving Wakefield at 6am and reaching London at 4pm the following day. In 1813 the *True Blue* left Wakefield at 5.30am for Manchester and Liverpool, reaching the latter at 8pm. Inside passengers paid 15s. An outside seat at the mercy of the elements cost 10s. Named with the patriotism of the time, the Waterloo began running from Wakefield to Leeds in 1814 leaving Wakefield at 9am and starting the return journey at 4pm. The 1822 directory shows that Wakefield was then connected by coach services to Halifax, Leeds, London, Manchester, Sheffield, and York. The *Mail* set out for London from the *Strafford Arms* at 9.30pm, the *Express* at 7.30pm. The *Union* left for Sheffield at 3pm. Those heading for Manchester could take the *Union* from the *Strafford Arms* at 6am. The *True Blue* went to Leeds at 5pm. From the *George* you could get the Harkforward coach to Halifax at 4pm and the *Prince Blucher* to York at 5pm. By 1829, thirty-eight bodies ran coaches or stage waggons to Birmingham, Doncaster, Grantham, Halifax, Huddersfield, Tadcaster, Sheffield and York.

The first public (horse) bus service in Wakefield came when Wakefield and District Omnibus Company was formed in 1890. By 1893, when it acquired a

Figure 38: A horse bus of *c.*1904. *The John Goodchild Collection*

charabanc to hold twenty-eight passengers, it had a stable of thirty-six horses and was running services to Lofthouse Gate, Sandal and Newmillerdam, Horbury, Agbrigg, Thornes and Calder Grove (Figure 38).

The railways

The first station serving Wakefield was on the North Midland Railway although at Oakenshaw it was some distance from the town. Railway travel came to Wakefield itself on 5 October 1840 with the opening of the Manchester and Leeds Railway which connected at Normanton with the North Midland Railway and ran west to Manchester. The area where Kirkgate Station was built had earlier been cultivated as strawberry gardens and orchards. By 1825 it had been taken over in part by Joseph Aspdin, a Leeds bricklayer who invented Portland Cement, and became the first cement works in the world. Aspdin moved to Ings Road to make way for the railway. The original station at Kirkgate was entirely functional and described by W S Banks as a 'cottage in size' Bennett's 'new and commodious omnibus' was available, passing through 'the principal streets' of the town to take passengers to and from Kirkgate Station for 4d (travelling outside) and 6d (in the comfort within). The Wakefield, Pontefract and Goole Railway opened its line from Kirkgate Station at the end of March 1848. Handsome new station buildings were provided in 1854.

The first direct route to Leeds was that of the Bradford, Wakefield and Leeds line, opened in 1857 with a station in a part of what had been John Milnes's mansion on the south side of Westgate. The principal feature of the line, in

Figure 39: Wakefield in the early twentieth century. The great railway viaduct can be seen in the middle distance. *The author's collection*

Figure 40: Westgate Station in the 1880s. *Yorkshire Archaeological Society*

Wakefield, remains the great 1,200 feet 95-arch viaduct (Figure 39). From 1 February 1866 the West Riding and Grimsby Railway provided a direct route from Westgate Station to London, meeting the Great Northern Railway at Doncaster. A new station was built the following year on the north side of Westgate, opening at the beginning of May (Figure 40). Despite having a tower, the station had no public clock until the late 1870s when Wakefield Tradesmen's Association complained about the lack.

New waiting rooms were built at the station in 1893 and a flight of steps was built from the western platform to Love Lane, where the prison is still sited, to make it easier to move the prisoners who were sent to Wakefield by train.

The impact of the railways was very considerable. Obviously they brought competition to the inland waterways but there was, for example, also an impact on hostelries: John Hewitt wrote of the number of butchers and dealers who, prior to the advent of rail travel, rode into Wakefield on the eve of cattle-market days:

> *These men entered the town from all sides and galloped their horses right to the respective inns at which they remained for the night to be in readiness for the market of the next day. They invariably came in bodies of tens, twenties and thirties as a check against highwaymen.*

Hewitt recalled the Town Crier in 1830 advising them to make the return journey in companies, again to deter the robbers who were known to be lying in wait.

The coming of the railways brought considerable expansion in the coalmining industry from the 1850s with many new collieries developing to the east of Wakefield in areas that had hitherto been agricultural. It also meant that different materials could be brought to Wakefield for road-making or building. Granite setts came from Scotland and Leicestershire to supplement the usual Elland Edge ones. Granite macadam from Darlington was ordered by Wakefield Corporation in the 1890s in quantities of 600 tons a time. This was then sprayed or brushed with tar.

Until the middle of the century, Westgate remained the home of some of the better-class families but the incursion of the railway drove them elsewhere.

By 1898 the waterways carried only the heaviest freight, in particular coal, lime and stone.

The banks
At the beginning of the nineteenth century, the only banks in Wakefield were the short-lived firm of John and William Shackleton, and that of Ingram, Kennett and Ingram. This failed in 1811. A further bank, with the name of Townend and Rishworth, was opened in 1802. When the London banking house of Boldero's failed in 1812, leading Wakefield businessmen advertised their faith in Townend and Rishworth but, ironically, this too failed and had to be wound up in 1814. A York bank, that of Wentworth and Chaloner, opened a branch in Wakefield, by 1815, taking Thomas Rishworth into partnership and adding the name of

Figure 41: The former Wakefield Savings Bank. *The author*

Rishworth to its title. Again it failed, this time in 1825 with a serious impact on Wakefield businesses. There was stability, however, with Leatham and Tew's bank which was established in Pontefract in 1801 and opened a Wakefield branch in 1809 on a site at the junction of Wood Street and Silver Street, buying the goodwill of Ingram, Kennet and Ingram's bank in its bankruptcy. An Act of Parliament of July 1817 to encourage the establishment of banks for savings amongst the 'industrious classes', prompted a public meeting in October, called by the Constable, to set up the Wakefield Savings Bank. In the patronising terms of the day, the meeting resolved that 'It is highly expedient that a bank be formed where the industrious of the lower orders may deposit their little savings with security and advantage'. In 1835 Bank House in Burton Street was built for it (Figure 41).

Further stability came with the founding of the Wakefield Banking Company in 1832. Eight years later it acquired the business of Beckett and Co of Barnsley thus becoming the Wakefield and Barnsley Union Bank. It occupied premises in Westgate. In 1877 a splendid new building was erected for it just a few doors higher up Westgate. After further changes it was absorbed into Barclay's Bank in 1923 (and the Westgate building was taken over by the ill-fated Wakefield Building Society). Leatham, Tew and Co built a new bank on their original site in 1880. It was amalgamated with Barclay's in 1906 (Figure 42). The Post Office Savings Bank was founded nationally in 1861. The Yorkshire Penny Bank, dating

Figure 42: Leatham Tew's Bank (on the right of the image), now Barclay's Bank, in 1885. *Yorkshire Archaeological Society*

from 1856, provided banking facilities at both the Church Institute and the Mechanics Institute but had no separate premises in Wakefield until the beginning of the twentieth century. The Wakefield and West Riding Building Society, with premises in Wood Street, was founded in 1846. Both the Leeds and County and the York City and County Bank acquired premises at the top of Westgate in the 1880s. The former was acquired by the London and Midland (later the Midland) Bank in 1890. The latter amalgamated with the London Joint Stock Bank in 1909 and this in turn amalgamated with the London and Midland Bank in 1918. The Midland Bank remained, and, as HSBC, remains on the same Westgate site as the former York City and County Bank. Its classical frontage was added in the 1920s.

Coalmining

Coal had been mined in the vicinity of Wakefield since (at least) Roman times. The possibility of water transport meant that seams accessible only by sinking deep shafts became economically viable and the industry saw substantial development from the early eighteenth century.

As early as 1745, Robert and William Wood advertised in *The York Courant* that they were bringing coals from Wakefield Outwood down a waggon way to a staith at Bottomboat.

From the end of the eighteenth century, coal was being shipped in quantity from staiths at Thornes Wharf, carried there from the Low Laithes and Kirkhamgate area by the parallel railways from Smithson's and Fenton's New Park collieries. From 1798, the Lake Lock railroad, the world's first public railway, had taken coal from collieries on the Outwood to the Aire and Calder Navigation north-east of Wakefield at Lake Lock. In 1837, 'great quantities' of coal were being sent to Hull, Selby and Gainsborough, and elsewhere. The first part of the Aire and Calder Navigation waggonway from Lofthouse Gate to Stanley Ferry, referred to locally as the Nagger line, opened in 1839. In 1854, the Denby Grange Colliery Railway brought coal to the Calder and Hebble Navigation at Calder Grove.

Ancillary industries developed to serve coal-mining. Fall Ing Foundry had been established in the 1787. Rope was needed for both vessels and collieries. There were earlier rope works in the Wakefield area but the largest rope-making firm to be established in the town was that of George Cradock, of 1853, which was later to become British Ropes.

The nineteenth century saw collieries developing close to the town to the north and the west. Westgate Common Colliery, sited close to what is today Lawefield Lane, was operating by 1792. Further west, Whinney Moor Colliery was in operation by 1819. The partnership there of Cookson and Co and Timothy Gomerson was dissolved in 1820. Lupset Colliery was in existence by 1830. Manor Colliery, just outside the borough boundary, developed on Cross Lane, between the Dewsbury and Horbury Roads, from 1847 and closed only in 1982

Figure 43: Manor Colliery shortly before its closure. *Wakefield MDC Cultural Services*

(Figure 43). For a time it had a Westgate Common pit close to the north side of Dewsbury Road which, from 1871, made use of the erstwhile Smithson's railway to take coal to Thornes Wharf. St John's Grove Colliery, situated in part where later a house was to be built for the Bishop of Wakefield, was operating from the 1830s with pits in the areas that are now Blenheim, Oxford and Richmond Roads and the Grammar School playing fields. From 1876 its extensive workings at Eastmoor were reached from the associated development, by the Victoria Coal Company, of Park Hill Colliery which survived until 1982. Again from at least the 1830s coal was mined on the Hatfeild Hall estate. *The Wakefield Herald* reported in 1837 that Fernandes, Dunn and Walker, who had recently bought Hatfeild Colliery, were preparing to open another colliery at Newton Lane End. They ran both under the unsurprising name of Victoria Collieries, obtaining leases from a variety of owners under contiguous estates and, working the Stanley Main and Shale seams and at least proving the Haigh Moor seam. They had wayleaves to take their coal from their pits, via their own waggonway to the Aire and Calder Navigation waggonway. Jose Luis Fernandes who with his sons, was in business as a corn factor, corn miller and wine merchant as well as colliery proprietor, became bankrupt in 1842 as did Richard Dunn. The Victoria Collieries were advertised for sale 'whole or in parts' in May 1843. In December the Limepit

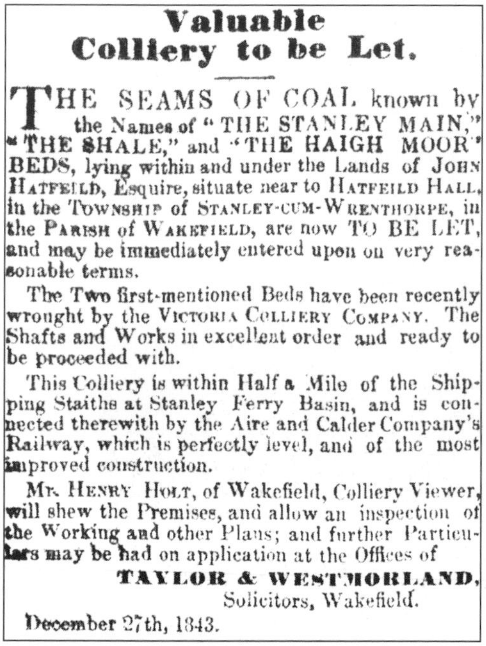

Valuable Colliery to be Let.

THE SEAMS OF COAL known by the Names of "THE STANLEY MAIN," "THE SHALE," and "THE HAIGH MOOR" BEDS, lying within and under the Lands of JOHN HATFEILD, Esquire, situate near to HATFEILD HALL, in the TOWNSHIP of STANLEY-CUM-WRENTHORPE, in the PARISH of WAKEFIELD, are now TO BE LET, and may be immediately entered upon on very reasonable terms.

The Two first-mentioned Beds have been recently wrought by the VICTORIA COLLIERY COMPANY. The Shafts and Works in excellent order and ready to be proceeded with.

This Colliery is within Half a Mile of the Shipping Staiths at Stanley Ferry Basin, and is connected therewith by the Aire and Calder Company's Railway, which is perfectly level, and of the most improved construction.

MR. HENRY HOLT, of Wakefield, Colliery Viewer, will shew the Premises, and allow an inspection of the Working and other Plans; and further Particulars may be had on application at the Offices of

TAYLOR & WESTMORLAND,
Solicitors, Wakefield.

December 27th, 1843.

Figure 44: Advertisement for the lease of Fernandes, Dunn and Walkers's Colliery near Hatfield Hall. *Wakefield M D Cultural Services*

Lane colliery was advertised alone (Figure 44). It was here on 4 March 1879 that sixteen men and six boys, and a number of horses lost their lives in an explosion at the Deep Drop pit. The colliery was owned at the time by Robert Hudson and Co. A little north of Newton Bar, between the Leeds and Bradford Roads, Daniel Micklethwaite had a colliery from the 1840s. In 1844, during a prolonged strike, his was the first concern to employ miners under the new terms demanded by the Miners' Union. At the time it was said that some 4,000 men from the Wakefield area were on strike. Micklethwaite's working miners contributed towards the strike funds. From the 1850s close to Balne Lane, the Balne Lane, California and Providence Collieries were developed. The equipment and machinery at Child and Barker's Balne Lane Colliery was advertised for sale in July 1852 and a lease of the colliery was available from that August. Joseph Marsland was in business as the New Victoria Colliery in Balne Lane by 1853. Subsequently he owned Providence Colliery. In 1851 an unnamed working colliery on the Snapethorpe Estate, where the Haigh Moor seam had been 'proved', was advertised to let. Roundwood Colliery, nearer to Flushdyke than Wakefield, opened in the early 1860s. A short-lived colliery on the Stanley Hall estate, opened in the 1870s by Robert Hudson, had pits close to the Wakefield Waterworks reservoir in Ouchthorpe Lane. The Victoria Coal Company took a lease of the coal under the grounds of the Pauper Lunatic Asylum in 1887.

Textiles

Wakefield's leading position in the wool and cloth marketing industries was lost in the first half of the nineteenth century. Baines's Directory of the West Riding of 1822 observed that Wakefield's trade in woollen stuffs had emigrated to Halifax and Bradford, and that there was scarcely a single woollen manufactory to be found. The 1834 Directory noted that Wakefield's wool market was 'of much less consequence' than it had been a few years since.

Until the first years of the nineteenth century, raw wool, was sold on market days at the top of Westgate. The early 1800s saw vast warehouses built for the wool-staplers. Cheapside, which had earlier been a yard, was laid out as a new street in 1801-2 and was, within twenty years, almost entirely flanked by

Figure 45: Joseph Jackson's warehouse. *The John Goodchild Collection*

warehouses. In King Street, which was laid out as a new street and adopted by the Street Commissioners as a public highway in 1801, still stands a four-storey warehouse which was built for Joseph Jackson about 1811 (Figure 45). There were a number of wool warehouses in Woolpacks Yard.

The 1805 directory lists thirty-one woolstaplers. By 1853 the figure was down to fifteen.

Various reasons (some unsupported and some demonstrably untrue) have been given for the decline in both the woolstapling and cloth trades. The Napoleonic blockade had injured the cloth trade, traders had been short-sighted in protecting their monopoly by, for example, excluding from the cloth hall all except those who had served their apprenticeship in Wakefield, former apprentices were banned from setting up their own business within seven miles of the town, merchants would take no apprentices unless they were close relatives, the aristocratic and merchant leaders of the town discouraged development, and the failure of the bank of Wentworth, Chaloner and Rishworth, in 1825, caused serious economic damage. The firm of J and J Naylor provides an example of both the backward-looking nature of the merchants and the damage done by the bank failure: the firm prospered under the traditional domestic system, buying unfinished cloth from Leeds or directly from home-based weavers; it was then finished at Naylors' and dyed at Holdsworth's. The bank failure caused its collapse.

Whilst domestic cloth weaving continued, white cloth was brought to Wakefield for dyeing. In the 1780s dyeworks on the River Calder just upstream from Wakefield were sold to the brothers Samuel and Joseph Holdsworth. For the first half of the nineteenth century their business expanded, weathering the general depression of 1825-6 and heavy losses caused by the failure of Wentworth, Chaloner and Rishworth's bank. Despite the increasing practice of textile manufacturers to dye their own cloth, the Holdsworths' successors continued in business until the early twentieth century. Halliley and Co had dyeworks at Westgate End/Chald Lane from at least 1805 until the middle of the century.

The first steam-powered mill in the Wakefield locality, supporting the local textile industry by scribbling and carding wool, had been built at Westgate Common, at the bottom of what is now Alverthorpe Road, in the 1780s by Ebenezer Aldred (c1745-1822). By 1805 it had been taken over by John Clarkson. One of the earliest steam-powered mills to have survived, at least as a building, into the twenty-first century, is Flanshaw Mill, which was opened by Thomas Ward (1775-1823) in 1808 again to support the hand-loom weaving industry by providing the complementary activities of processing raw wool and by fulling, or felting, the woven cloth. The beck provided water for the steam engine and, later, for dyeing. As the handloom industry declined, the mill went over to worsted spinning.

From the 1820s Wakefield saw a rise in the worsted spinning industry, made possible by steam power and which accelerated in the 1860s. The pioneer was Thomas Marriott who had begun business at Westgate End before 1800 but who then built an immense mill in 1822-23. One of the longest-surviving concerns was that of George Lee which was established at Westgate End in 1830 and closed only in 1987. William Marsland had set himself up as a worsted manufacturer in New Street by 1830. In the 1840s and 50s he continued worsted and woollen spinning in Kirkgate and Brunswick Street.

Balne Mill was built in 1837-8 by Tottenham Lee and a part of it was taken by J L Fernandes and Richard Dunn (Figure 46). Writing in March 1837 with considerable optimism about the state of the town's economy, the editor of *The Wakefield Herald* spoke of the progress in erecting the new mill at Balne Field, and noted that Messrs Graham were building saw mills in Thornes Lane, and John and William Young were erecting starch works at Primrose Hill. Balne Mill was, however, advertised to let in 1842 after the failure of Fernandes and Dunn. Edward Beet Metcalf had a mill with a 20hp engine in Back Lane in 1850. The

Figure 46: Balne Mill. *The author*

1853 directory lists twenty-five firms engaged in worsted or woollen yarn spinning. A further mill was established on a site between the bottom of Westgate and Ings Road by Matthew Porrit Stonehouse in the mid 1850s.

So extensive was the industry in the 1860s, and so quickly growing, that in 1864 George Horridge extolled it in an essay in his *Almanack*. He wrote of the 'considerable and visible expansion' referring to 'the large worsted mill of Messrs Lee and Sons in Westgate, and that of Messrs Fallon and Watmough in Back Lane.' Marriotts had greatly enlarged their Westgate mills and taken over the Balne Lane mill. New mills had been erected in Primrose Hill, Wood Street, Balne Lane and Alverthorpe Road. Joseph Wade had changed Portobello Mills to a woollen cloth manufactory 'employing a large number of hands'. The Tammy Hall had been transformed into a worsted mill. Horridge referred also to new chemical works, the machine shop of Milner and son in Alverthorpe Road, a flour mill built by Howarth and White, Mr Whitham's extensive forge by the Calder employing over 250 men, and Mr Cordingley's engine shop in Thornhill Street. He commented that Wakefield was attracting industrialists from elsewhere, Joseph Wade from Morley, Samuel Whitham from Leeds, and Fallon and Watmough from Manchester.

In 1868 there was a two-column editorial in *The Wakefield Express*. This described worsted spinning as 'one of the most flourishing and important branches of commerce'. It extolled the achievements of R H Barker and Co, Isaac Briggs and Son, Fallon and Shaw, J Goldthorp and Co, George Lee and Sons, J Marriott at St John's, T Marriott and Son, J Moorhouse, and M P Stonehouse. The two last firms manufactured carpet yarn as well as knitting worsteds. Firms were now able to undertake every process from taking in the raw wool to turning out and marketing the finished product, including washing, drying, carding, spinning and dyeing. Both George Lee's and R H Barker's had used the

distinguished Bradford practice of Lockwood and Mawson for their recent
extensions, the latter mill being provided with the flourish of ornamental
campanile towers. Briggs's four-storey Rutland Mill of 1870, close to Wakefield
Bridge, was designed by the local architect, William Watson. In August 1872,
when it was largely destroyed by fire, Briggs and Son, who were transferring their
operation to the new mill on the south bank of the river, also had the mill in Back
Lane where combing, carding and spinning took place. It lay immediately to the
west of the railway line and it was thought to have been a spark from an engine
that set it ablaze.

The worsted-spinning firm of Tom and Henry Harrap moved in 1890 from
Horbury to a mill of the 1790s at Alverthorpe, naming their complex Bective
Mills.

There was never an extensive cloth-manufacturing industry in Wakefield. The
first firm was that of Joseph Wade and Son, founded at Portobello Mill in 1861.
John Samuel Booth began cloth manufacturing at Castle Bank Mills in 1869.
George and James Stubley, who built the Calder Mills in 1876, also wove cloth.
In 1900, when there was a fire there, the Stubleys employed some 700
workpeople. They lost 103 looms, fourteen spinning frames and eleven mules. At
the time they also owned Bottom Mills at Batley and it was said that materials
were transported from one site to the other daily by a powerful traction engine.

The Mungo and Shoddy trade developed in Dewsbury and Batley rather than
in Wakefield but in the 1880s for example Joseph Salkeld had a shoddy mill in
Chald Lane The linen industry was primarily a Barnsley one but a flax mill in
Kirkgate was offered for sale in 1817 and there was for a time a flax mill in Back
Lane which was occupied by Messrs Rouse until 1842.

The textile industry prompted another trade: in 1849 a firm was established at
Westgate Common to recover grease, by evaporation, from the liquid produced
by the washing of worsted at the local mills. This was then passed on to the soap-
making industry. The resultant smell was said to be sickening and nauseous and
to remind of 'burnt treacle spiced with asafoetida and buttered with train oil'. The
business, which became Teall and Simpson's, moved to Warehouse Yard close to
Wakefield Bridge which became commonly known as 'Grease Hole Yard'. In
1860, William Teall patented an improved method of extracting fats and oily
matters from the wash water.

The markets

Wakefield market was of sufficiently ancient origin to have preceded any formal
charter but was the province of the Lord of the Manor. On Fridays, livestock,
farm produce, earthenware and other goods were sold in the open streets about
the Bull Ring, or Market Place as it was called. The corn market was on the north
side of the top of Westgate. Corn was sold by sample or sack, in the open street,
whatever the weather. The market was opened and closed by the ringing of a bell.
Once closed, the corn had to be immediately moved from the street. Distinct

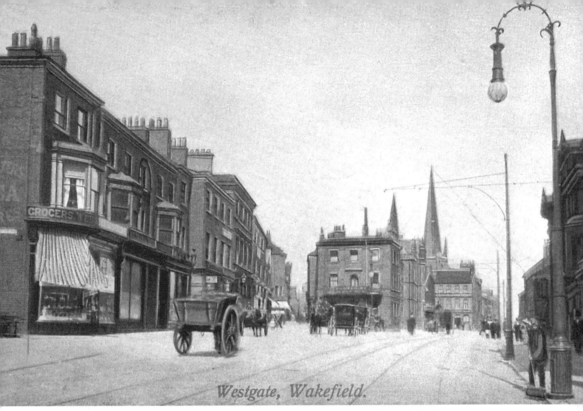

Figure 47: Westgate in the early years of the twentieth century. The original corn exchange is in the centre of the picture. *The author's collection*

areas, marked out by wooden posts, were allocated to wheat, oats, rye and beans. The waterway connections between Wakefield and the agricultural areas to the east on the one hand and, on the other, the grain-hungry markets to the west, led to its becoming one of the major corn markets in the country. The growth in the corn trade began, effectively, in the 1790s when the brothers Thomas and John Tootal set up in business with corn warehouses at Thornes Wharf. The nuisance of wet weather, the crowding of an area shared with cattle, sheep and geese, and the increase in trade led to the opening of the first Corn Exchange, at the top of Westgate in 1820 (Figure 47). Built by banker Thomas Rishworth, the site was repossessed in 1825, by Rishworth's landlords the Trustees of Kirkburton School, when the bank of Wentworth, Chaloner and Rishworth failed. The rival Leeds Corn Exchange was built in 1826-8.

By 1836, the corn dealers were determined to have again their own exchange building. The existing Corn Trade Committee was augmented, shares in a projected company were offered for sale, and there was a quest for a suitable site at a viable price. The possibility of building in Kirkgate was mooted – it was close to the waterway and, with the likelihood of a railway crossing it and degrading the environment, property would be quite cheap. But the area on Westgate, lying between Queen Street and Market Street, was preferred; it was closer to 'respectable' inns, to the banking houses, and to the post office. Initial plans were drawn up by a young Wakefield architect, William Billinton for a most ambitious edifice. The Wakefield Corn Exchange Company was founded in March 1837. In

Figure 48: The Corn Exchange of 1838. *The author's collection*

the event the company chose a less costly (but only a little less impressive) design by William Lambie Moffat of Doncaster. The laying of the foundation stone, done with full Masonic honours, was a splendid event. It took place on 24 May 1837, chosen because it was the birthday of the heir to the throne, Princess Victoria. There was a procession from the Court House in Wood Street to Westgate, with the Constable and Deputy Constables, members of the Wakefield Masonic Lodge of Unanimity, senior figures from amongst Masons in the West Riding Province, shareholders in the Company, and the Provincial Grand Master, the Earl of Mexborough. Borne on velvet cushions in the procession were silver cups filled with wine and oil, a cornucopia filled with corn, and the Masons' symbolic tools, their plumb, square and compasses. The Earl laid the stone, and checked it with the tools. The oil, wine and corn were poured or scattered over it. The Reverend Dr Martin Naylor, as Provincial Chaplain, made a speech. There was a dinner in the evening at the *Great Bull Hotel*. The Exchange floor was opened for business in January 1838 (Figure 48). The Company advertised that it has spacious vaults to be let which included counting houses, packing houses and 'other conveniences'. The Guardians of the Poor Law Union had their Board Room in the Corn Exchange until the new workhouse was built in 1852.

An extension to the Corn Exchange, providing a larger exchange floor, was opened in 1864 when the weekly business was said to amount to £50,000. The corn trade continued throughout the century to be very important. In 1904 it was described as the 'chief support of the town'.

Although livestock sales continued to take place in the street in the town centre for the first half of the nineteenth century, a fortnightly cattle-market established by the Governors of the Wakefield Charities in 1765, grew to be the largest in the north of England. John Bigland reported in 1812 that graziers and jobbers from Lincolnshire, the East Riding, and Craven, brought their livestock there and the beasts were bought by butchers from Halifax, Huddersfield, Sheffield and Manchester.

The Cattle Market lying between the Ings Road and George Street, or Fair Ground Road as it was termed, expanded in 1827 following the creation of the Denby Dale turnpike road (Figure 49). Livestock was brought, on foot, from considerable distances, including from Hull and Liverpool, and then pastured in fields on the outskirts of the town to fatten up. Three inns had dedications to the Graziers. It is no doubt significant that when the *George Hotel* was to let in 1838, its owner advertised that the tenant could also have twenty acres of grassland close to the town. The need for grazing land was such that when farms at Crofton were advertised to let in 1827 they were said to be 'advantageously situated for graziers and dealers in cattle frequenting the great cattle fairs in Wakefield'. In 1837 it was noted that as many as 1,000 head of cattle of 13,000 sheep might be penned on a single day. The market was held fortnightly until 1849 when,

Figure 49: Wakefield Cattle Market. *The author's collection*

Figure 50: The Borough Market in the 1880s. *Yorkshire Archaeological Society*

presumably because of increased demand and the increasing numbers of beasts brought by rail, it was held weekly.

Transport by rail brought its own problems, not least in the delay of some of the trains and the charge made for cleaning the cattle trucks. To negotiate with the railway companies a Cattle Dealers and Graziers Association was formed in January 1888 with its headquarters in Wakefield.

In the 1890s the annual Christmas Fat Cattle Market saw beasts brought from both Ireland and Scotland with buyers from way beyond Yorkshire and cattle and sheep worth over £62,000 sold in a single day. At the Inquiry in 1895 into the proposed extension to the municipal borough, sales were said to average 1,400 cattle and 4,000 sheep a week.

Market trading was cleared from the streets when the Borough Market opened in 1851 (Figure 50). The Borough Market Company was formed in 1847, incorporated by an act of Parliament which allowed for the purchase of the fair and market rights of the Manor of Wakefield and of a swathe of the town immediately to the north-east of the Bull Ring. The property concerned lay in Union Street, Nelson Street, New Street, Union Foundry Yard, Smallpage Yard and Northgate. It included three public houses, the *Griffin Inn* in Northgate, the *Carriers Arms* in New Street, and the *Free Masons Arms*, many cottages and their pig styes, ashpits and manure heaps. It would, in fact, have rid Wakefield of some wretched slums. A second Act, in 1850, enabled the company instead to buy land to the south-east of the town centre that formed part of the Rectory Manor estate, to widen Vicarage Lane and to form new streets which were named after key figures in the scheme. The change of location was, fruitlessly, opposed by some of the townspeople as being at too great a distance from Wakefield's centre. The narrow Parsonflatte running from the Bull Ring, was widened, giving ready access, and renamed Westmorland Street, after J J Westmorland, the company's lawyer. Teall Street was created giving access to the market area from Kirkgate. The Goody Bower was re-routed and became Brook Street. The market hall was built in 1851 and the market itself opened to the public on 29 August of that year. The Company made it clear that anyone exposing goods for sale in the streets would be prosecuted. The first case was brought against John Vaux, a grocer in Westgate in September 1851.

Wakefield had four fair days, on 4 and 5 July and on 11 and 12 November. The first and third of these were for the sale of horses and cattle, the second is described as a 'toy fair', and the fourth was the hiring fair, where servants and farm workers could be taken on for a year at a time. The fairs were moved to the area of the Borough Market in 1851.

Writing in 1871, W S Banks commented that the market 'though one of the sights of Wakefield, cannot by even a favourable apologist, be called a pleasant sight. It has a paltry market house, and the ground is unpaved, dirty and disagreeable.'

The old Market Cross was taken down in 1866 and sold in pieces. One of its pillars stands in the garden of the Art Gallery in Wentworth Terrace (Figure 51).

Figure 51: A pillar from the Market Cross. *The author*

The Borough Market Company was sold in 1875 to Benjamin Shaw of Cowick Hall, Snaith. At the close of the century arrangements were in hand for Wakefield Corporation to buy it.

Some other industries and enterprises

Wakefield enjoyed the enterprise of a number of pioneers of industry. Joseph Rhodes began the still-surviving machine-making firm in Wakefield Ings in 1824; it moved to Elm Tree Street, Belle Vue, in 1921. Joseph Aspdin (1778-1855), from Leeds, the inventor of Portland Cement, founded his cement works in Lower

Kirkgate in 1825. Charles Clay (1830-1897) moved his agricultural implement manufactory from Oakenshaw to the Stennard Island at Wakefield Bridge in 1861. John Kilner and Sons of Thornhill, makers of glass carboys and bottles, extended their operation to Wakefield when they acquired the Ebenezer Glass Bottle works in Calder Vale Road in 1867. In 1878, Manchester-born Edward Allen Brotherton (1856-1930), began to produce ammonia at neighbouring premises in Calder Vale Road, going on to make a range of coal-tar products. Edward Simpson (1843-1914) who lived for some years at Walton Hall, joined W T Hodgson who had set up a soap works at Walton in 1818, and, after a series of lawsuits because of its polluting the Walton atmosphere, moved it to the site of the former Calder Dyeworks at Thornes in 1851 where the cliffs of black ash, from the residue from the soap-making process, still stand beside the river near Denby Dale Road. The business was sold in the early twentieth century to Lever Brothers. Edward Green (1799-1865) who patented his fuel economiser in 1845, commenced his engineering firm in Kirkgate in 1821, moving to premises in Westgate and then Ings Road, before settling in 1861 in Calder Vale Road. Richard Bradley founded the engineering firm which subsequently became Bradley and Craven, in Dewsbury Road in 1843. The firm made colliery winding engines and brick-making machines. In 1897, William Garforth founded the Diamond Coal Cutting Company, with premises on Stennard Island, to manufacture coal-cutting machinery under licence from Richard Sutcliffe.

Commercial brewing had begun in Wakefield by 1781 when Robert Harrison had premises in Red Lion Yard, Kirkgate. The firm lasted, through three generations, until 1839. Thomas Carter's Victoria Brewery, in Fairground Road, where he built a handsome house, opened in 1846. The company amalgamated with Melbourne Brewery, Leeds, in 1889. Brewing continued on the site until the early 1920s. Beverley's Eagle Brewery, founded in Harrison Street in 1861 survived until 1968, having built up a chain of 173 public houses. In 1872, George Newton, who had earlier had Phoenix Brewery, founded the Crown Brewery, in Providence Place off Kirkgate. In 1886 it was taken over by Walker and Co. The business, which then included nineteen public houses, was put up for auction in 1922 and the brewery closed. Fernandes' Old Bridge Brewery was established alongside Fall Ing cut in 1850 by the brothers Jose Luis junior and Noel Luis Fernandes, members of the family that had held the lease of Wakefield's soke mill and had been involved too in coal mining.

Pop – aerated mineral water – was introduced to Wakefield in the 1860s by Edward Pearson Shaw (1828-1880) who had set up in business as a chemist and druggist in the Bull Ring in 1854.

There had been unsuccessful co-operative societies in Wakefield in the 1830s but two founded in the 1860s, the Wakefield Industrial and the Wakefield Borough Co-operative Societies lasted well into the second half of the twentieth century. The Societies both sprang from the interest amongst prison officers in the comparatively low cost of food when it was bought on a large scale for the

Figure 52: Unity House, built for the Wakefiield Industrial Co-operative Society in 1901.
The author

prison. The prison governor, chaplain and accountant all supported the formation of a co-operative society for the wider public. The Wakefield Industrial Society was formed in 1867 with premises in Bank Street. In 1876 substantial new premises were built in Bank Street to the design of W and D Thornton. The vast extension later known as Unity House was added in 1901 (Figure 52). A rival Society, the Wakefield Borough, was formed at the same time. A less well documented Westgate Common Co-operative Society had 111 members in 1871 and was looking for a site for a building.

The Wakefield printing, publishing and bookselling firm of William Nicholson and sons was an internationally successful pioneer of cheap books. It had first been established in Halifax in 1828 but moved to the purpose-built Albion Works in Jacobs Well Lane in 1871. The premises were designed by William Crutchley. Among other books published by the firm were its Wakefield Juvenile Series at a shilling each and its Cottagers' Library at the same price. The former included *The Vicar of Wakefield* and *Notable Battles of England*, whilst the latter included the *Awful Disclosures of Maria Monk* and *Six Months in a Convent*. William Nicholson junior, the more active of the two sons, who ran the business after his father's death in 1875, was a radical in politics and a Baptist in religious adherence. Religious works were among the firm's publications.

As elsewhere, a local committee, including aldermen and councillors, representatives of the committee of the Mechanics Institution, and manufacturers, was established in January 1850 to promote the Great Exhibition of 1851 in which some Wakefield firms took part. They included L F Bauwen of the Grease Works who showed pure oil and grease extracted from the soap refuse from textile (and other) mills, Edward Green (the fuel economiser), Richard Bradley (a machine for making bricks), the quarrymaster Samuel Seal (scythe stones and grind stones), J Holdsworth (pieces of stuff), Marriott and Son (knitting worsted) and Richard Poppleton (knitting worsted). A model of a working colliery, made by local miners, was also submitted.

Wakefield had its own 'Great Exhibition' in 1865. The Industrial and Fine Art Exhibition originated with the then vicar of Wakefield, Charles E Camidge, who proposed a modest exhibition 'to encourage the industry and useful employ of the children connected with the parish church schools'. The idea snowballed. By January 1865 the purpose of the exhibition had become 'to encourage the industry of Wakefield'. A purpose-built exhibition hall, designed by William Watson, was erected on the vacant site in Wood Street where the Town Hall was later to be built. (Figure 53). The nearby and recently-vacated Tammy Hall was also used. The exhibition was an immense success – financially as well as educationally and socially. It opened on 30 August 1865 and closed only on 19 October. Some 189,423 admissions were recorded. Wakefield's industrial and commercial businesses contributed as did local individuals of every class and sphere.

J Rhodes and Son, E Green and Son, and Hodgson and Simpson all exhibited their products at the Paris international exhibition in 1867.

At the end of the century *The Wakefield Journal* was able to refer to Wakefield having its share in the national prosperity. By now the coal trade was regarded as the staple trade of the district. Among the most prosperous companies at the time were Edmund Green's ('going flat out night and day'), E A Brotherton's, and the Seamless Steel Boat Company, which had been founded in 1892 and had many overseas customers. George Cradock's had just enlarged their premises. The woollen industry was surviving primarily on government orders and the decline

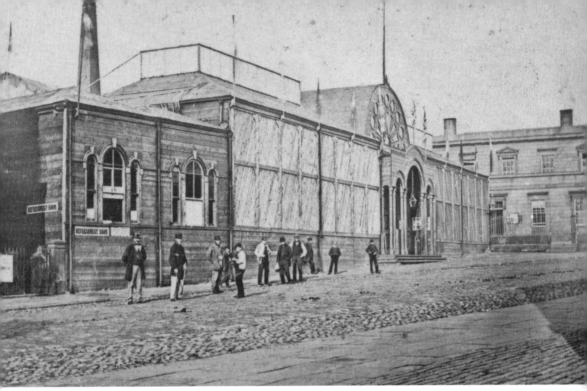

Figure 53: The Exhibition Hall designed by William Watson for the Wakefield Industrial and Fine Art Exhibition of 1865. *The John Goodchild Collection*

Figure 54: Jackson's Arcade. *The John Goodchild Collection*

in hand knitting was having an adverse impact on wool and worsted spinning. However in 1896 the cloth trade was described as 'one of the most important branches of Wakefield industry' with a large number of hands employed at Colbeck's mill in Alverthorpe, G and J Stubley's Calder Mills, W Wade and Sons' Portobello Mills, and J S Booth's Castle Bank Mills.

The century ended with a retail innovation. Jackson's of Leeds announced plans for an arcade in Kirkgate on the site formerly of the office of the West Riding Surveyor (Figure 54).

Sources

Holden's Triennial Directory for 1805.

John Goodchild, *Wakefield and Wool.*

J Aikin, *A description of the Country from Thirty to Forty Miles round Manchester*, London, 1795.

John Goodchild, *Our Industrial Heritage*, 1977.

Kate Taylor, (ed), *Wakefield District Heritage*, 1976.

George Tyas, *The Battles of Wakefield*, 1854.

George Horridge, *Wakefield Almanack.*

K A Cowlard, *The Urban Development of Wakefield 1801-1901*, unpublished thesis, 1974

John Goodchild, 'The Story of Rhubarb' in *Aspects of Wakefield*, Volume 1, 1998

John Goodchild, 'City prospered as an important inland port', *The Wakefield Express*, 21 January 1983.

John Goodchild, *Attorney at Large: the concerns of John Lee of Wakefield 1759-1836*, 1986.

Eric Rape, 'The Chain Bridge', *Wakefield Historical Society Journal*, Vol 10, 1983.

John Goodchild, *A Wakefield Town Trail*, 1980.

L S Pressnell and John Orbell, *A Guide to the Historical Records of British Banking*, 1985.

John Goodchild, *The Coal Kings of Yorkshire*, 1978

John Goodchild, *Wakefield's First Railway and its Collieries*, 2002.

John Goodchild, *The Lake Lock Railway*, 1977.

John Goodchild, *A New History of Caphouse Colliery*, 2000.

John Goodchild, Unpublished notes

John Goodchild, 'Dyeing for Wakefield', in *Aspects of Wakefield*, Volume 2, 1999.

Henry Clarkson, *Memories of Merry Wakefield*, 1887.

John Goodchild, 'Wakefield Corn Exchange', in *Wakefield Historical Society Journal* Volume 12, 2001.

George Horridge, *Wakefield Almanack*, 1864.

John Bigland, *The Beauties of England and Wales*, Vol XVI, London, 1812.

British Universal Directory, 1793-1798, Facsimile text, 1993.

E Green, and Son, *Waste not, Want Not*, 1956.

True North Books, *More Memories of Wakefield*, 1999.

John Goodchild, 'When the city got a taste for brewing', *The Wakefield Express*, 2 October 1993.

John Goodchild, 'Brewing in Wakefield' in *Aspects of Wakefield*, Volume 3, 2001.

Peter Wood, 'Wakefield goes pop', unpublished essay.

Charles E Camidge, *A History of Wakefield and its Industrial and Fine Arts Exhibition*, 1866.

$\mathscr{R}$ELIGION: GROWTH, CONCERN AND CONFLICT

Nineteenth century Wakefield, like the rest of the country, saw a substantial increase in the number of Christian places of worship. It saw, too, perennial endeavours to promote religion amongst the working classes. And it saw controversy and friction when the Established Church was divided between evangelicalism and ritualism, when Nonconformity opposed the Established Church, and when some factions condemned Popery.

The ecclesiastical parish of Wakefield was considerably larger than the township and included the townships of Alverthorpe with Thornes, Horbury, and Stanley cum Wrenthorpe. At the beginning of the nineteenth century it was bounded by the parishes of Rothwell, Methley, Sandal, Thornhill, Dewsbury and East Ardsley. Until 1836 it lay in the diocese of York. It became a part of the Diocese of Ripon when it was created by Order in Council on 5 October 1836. By the end of the century it was at the centre of the diocese of Wakefield and its parish church was a cathedral.

In 1801 there were only two Anglican churches in Wakefield itself – the parish church and the recently built church of St John the Baptist, the centre piece of the handsome 1790s St John's Square (Figure 55). St John's became a parish in

Figure 55: St John's Church in the 1880s. *Yorkshire Archaeological Society*

Figure 56: St Peter and St Leonard's, Horbury. *The author*

its own right in 1844. Horbury had had a chapel of ease since at least medieval times, the ancient one being replaced by one designed and financed by its own distinguished architect, John Carr, in 1794 (Figure 56). Sandal, which became a part of the municipal borough of Wakefield only in 1909, was a distinct parish and had its own medieval church. The Nonconformist places of worship were more numerous. The Unitarian Chapel in Westgate had been built in 1751-2. The Wesleyan Methodists' meeting house in Thornhill Street was opened in 1774. The Independents (later termed the Congregationalists and later still the United Reformed Church) had opened their first Wakefield chapel, Zion, on the back lane which was later to be called George Street in 1783. A second Independent congregation, started by disaffected members of Zion, had begun meeting in 1799 in the new Assembly Rooms in Crown Court. The Society of Friends had a meeting house at Belle Vue, an area again absorbed into the municipal borough of Wakefield only in 1909.

Nonconformity in its varied forms
In the nineteenth century, Nonconformity continued to expand through the emergence of new branches, the setting up of mission chapels, or the secession of

members of an existing congregation. The 1851 Religious Census revealed that in Wakefield more people then attended Nonconformist places of worship than those of the Established Church. Nonconformist men were among the leading figures in the town in terms of both their professional, commercial or industrial success and their influence in the public sphere.

The first chapel of the new century was Salem, a substantial building opened in George Street in 1801 for the Assembly Rooms Independent congregation. A mission chapel cum school was established on the Wakefield-Aberford Road, at Eastmoor, in 1811. It was rebuilt in 1872. Salem closed in the early 1930s, was sold to Wakefield Corporation in 1935 and was used during the Second World War as a British restaurant.

Much of the chapel-building was by one or other of the diverse Methodist groups. West Parade, a handsome building designed to hold 1,500 people, which replaced the Wesleyans' Thornhill Street Chapel, was opened in 1801. The Society of Friends then took over the Thornhill Street building and, although now in a twentieth-century meeting house of 1965, remains on the same site in the twenty-first century.

The West Parade congregation was responsible for founding two further Wesleyan chapels in Wakefield with the opening of the first at Eastmoor in 1822 and the second at Westgate End, where there had been a preaching station from 1813, in 1828.

Primitive Methodists (sometimes called Ranters) were an offshoot of Wesleyan Methodism. The movement was founded in Staffordshire by Hugh Bourne (1772-1852) after he had been expelled from the Wesleyan Methodist Society in 1808 for holding outdoor, day-long, revival meetings which were not approved by the Methodist 'establishment'. The name of the breakaway group is thought to derive from its members' wish to return to the 'true', original form of Methodism. They emphasised simplicity in their chapel buildings and in their manner of worship and their principal adherents were in rural communities or amongst the working class. There were Primitive Methodist meetings in a house in Quebec Street, Wakefield, in 1810. Their first chapel was built there in 1822-3 and at least by 1833 was known as Ebenezer Chapel. It was advertised for sale in 1834 as part of the estate of Lucy Lumb (she had acquired it in 1833). It measured fifty-six foot by forty-two foot and had galleries. From April 1836 it was, for seven years, home to the Baptists. At much the same time a subscription list was formed to raise funds for a new Primitive Methodist chapel. This was to be Ebenezer Chapel in Market Street which opened in 1838. When it was first built, the Market Street Chapel was 'unsightly and uncomfortable'. It had a high gallery, box pews, an organ loft and an awkward stairway to the pulpit. Its basement Sunday School was 'low and dingy' and was only eight feet in height.

By 1821 a Primitive Methodist Society was established at New Scarborough. A chapel was built in Regent Street, off Alverthorpe Road, in 1874.

A little-known-about Primitive Methodist Society was established at Newmillerdam in 1822. The Chapel which was built there in 1880 owes its origins, however, to a group which broke away from the Wesleyan Chapel nearby in the late 1860s. Services were held for some years in a cottage in Almshouse Lane, Newmillerdam, but sufficient funds were raised for the foundation stone of the new chapel to be laid in 1879. The increasing development of the Belle Vue area led to a mission chapel cum Sunday School being established there in 1777. The generosity of local quarry owner Samuel Seal enabled the erection of a chapel and Sunday School which opened on 23 January 1888 under the wing of Ebenezer Chapel in Market Street.

The congregation of Bethel Free Church Methodist Chapel in Thornes Lane was founded in the 1840s by the Wakefield Town Mission on a river boat named *Bethel* moored at Thornes Wharf. In 1853 the boat began to leak so badly that the boatkeeper had to keep pumping it out during services. For the next three years services were held instead in a sail loft. But George William Harrison, who had been the first Mayor of Wakefield in 1848, built premises for the congregation at his own expense. The new building was opened on 27 March 1856. After Harrison's death in 1860 his widow continued to allow the use of the premises free of charge. Funds were raised to build a permanent chapel and to buy the old building in 1869-70.

In 1853 the Wesleyan Reformers were meeting in a room in the Corn Exchange. There was another group of Reformers at Eastmoor. They built the United Free Methodist Chapel in Market Street in 1858. A second chapel, Brunswick Chapel in Saville Street, was opened in 1876.

Grove Road Chapel, converted in the twenty-first century into flats, was opened on 15 February 1866 for the Methodist New Connexion. It was designed in a pointed Italian style by William Hill of Leeds and built by the Wakefield firm of Latham. It had a gallery on three sides and a larger room and two classrooms for Sunday School use in the basement. The pulpit was very large and was described at the time of opening by a reporter from *The Wakefield Free Press* as providing 'ample scope for a display of muscular Christianity'! The group, led by Alexander Kilham, had broken away from Wesleyan Methodism in 1797. The Wakefield members had, prior to the chapel's opening, maintained 'a struggling but energetic' presence in Wakefield in a room which had formerly been a casino. The chapel closed in 1978.

The congregation at Salem Chapel seems to have been prone to secession. A short-lived Independent congregation was founded in Quebec Street in 1829 when, the Reverend Dr Richard Cope resigned from Salem, where, he said he had for five years 'patiently endured a series of troubles and difficulties'. Some of his well wishers negotiated the use of the Primitive Methodist Chapel. His first service there was 19 July. There were twenty-six people at a communion service on 6 September 1829 and the congregation grew to number eighty. However, Cope observed, the chapel was 'in a bad situation' and the rent was 'burdensome'.

Figure 57: Zion Chapel in George Street. *Yorkshire Archaeological Society*

How, or whether, Cope's followers shared the chapel with the Primitive Methodists is unclear. Their use of the chapel ended, as did that of the Primitive Methodists, early in 1836 when it was sold as part of the estate of Lucy Lumb.

There was another secession at Salem in 1848 when minister, William Lamb, resigned and took some of the congregation with him when he began conducting services in the Music Saloon. A further Independent Chapel was opened at John Street in 1874, apparently by disaffected people from Salem.

The Independents at Zion rebuilt their George Street chapel in 1843-4. It was designed by one of their trustees, William Shaw, who lived at the time at Portobello but who later moved to Stanley Hall (Figure 57). The chapel was relinquished only in 2002. Zion established mission rooms in working-class districts at Mark Street, Thornes, and in the 1870s at Primrose Hill.

Flanshaw gained a Nonconformist chapel when the owner of Flanshaw Mill, William Oakes, determined to 'do something' for the district. His foreman, John Fothergill, suggested that he build a chapel. Built, in a Gothic style, with stone

Figure 58: The former Baptist Chapel in George Street. *Simon Jenkins*

from a quarry just to the north of it, it was opened in 1866. Some of its fittings came from the one-time Primitive Methodist Chapel in Quebec Street. It remained for many years in private ownership albeit used for public worship. Oakes himself died in 1871 and was buried in front of the building. It was subsequently let to trustees and was handed to the Yorkshire Congregational Union in 1920.

The Baptists had no chapel in Wakefield until they opened the erstwhile Primitive Methodist Quebec Street chapel in April 1836. Prior to that there had been meetings of members of the denomination in 1812 in a school room in Hardy Croft and in 1818 in the Assembly Rooms in Crown Court. The first service in Quebec Street was taken by Dr Steadman, one-time theological tutor at Horton College, Bradford, and for some time afterwards services were conducted by Horton College students. Their chapel in George Street, looking onto the Cattle Market, was opened in 1844 (Figure 58).

It is not clear when the Salvation Army first began activities in Wakefield. However, it certainly held a service in the theatre on 12 June 1882 although in 1893, when General Booth first visited Wakefield, it was said that the Wakefield Corps had been established only seven years previously. At Christmas 1887 its members 'had a tremendous march' around the town and provided free ham teas for 340 people. In 1893 it was operating from premises in Thompson's Yard. There was a problem in finding a meeting place for the General's visit. West Parade Wesleyans, with the largest chapel in the town centre, refused to host the event, evidently fearing that the working people who would attend would damage their 'sumptuous' furnishings. The meeting was held in the United Methodist Free Church in Market Street. Its first barracks were in the old Independent school room at Eastmoor. The Army's open-air meetings in the Market Place (the Bull Ring) prompted a petition to Wakefield Council in 1897 from owners of property there who described the Army's activities as 'obstructive and in many ways unpleasant, undesirable and unnecessary'.

A sect calling itself simply the Christian Church met between the 1860s and 1880s in Queen Street. There was a fire there in January 1887 but the contemporary reports provide no further details of the sect.

The eccentric Christian Israelite leader John Wroe (1782-1863), for whom Melbourne House at Wrenthorpe was built, had a chapel for his sect in the middle years of the century, in Crown Court.

There were branches of the Spiritualist Church in Wakefield by 1893 when they were meeting in Barstow Square and Baker's Yard, Kirkgate. (The first Spiritualist Church was established at Keighley in 1853.)

The Anglican churches

The first new Anglican churches, within the parish of Wakefield but outside the township, and built as 'chapels of ease', were financed, at least in part, from the 'Million Fund' – the £1m set aside by Parliament in 1818, following the Battle of Waterloo, from the indemnity paid by Austria. There were three of them and, like other churches of the period, they were 'inevitably governed by the requirement of as many sittings as possible for as little money as possible'. The foundation stone of St Peter's, Stanley, was laid on 13 September 1822 and the church was consecrated on 6 September 1824 (Figure 59). At Alverthorpe, the foundation stone of St Paul's was laid on 12 March 1823 and it was consecrated on 1 July 1825 (Figure 60). St James's Church, Thornes, was built a little later and with a grant of only £1,000 from the Million Fund. Most of the cost was borne by Benjamin Gaskell and his wife of Thornes House. The foundation stone was laid by James Milnes Gaskell, the son of the benefactor, on 6 August 1829, and the church was consecrated by the Archbishop of York on 12 October 1831 (Figure 61).

Figure 59: St Peter's Church, Stanley. *Yorkshire Archaeological Society*

The three churches were radically different in design although all coming from the same practice of Atkinson and Sharp of York. The Wakefield historian John Walker described Stanley Church as 'a most unsatisfactory edifice' and explained that the architecture was imposed by the Ecclesiastical Commissioners in opposition to plans approved by the Vicar of Wakefield, Samuel Sharp. It has two western towers, open battlements, crocketed pinnacles and high walls with large perpendicular windows. Alverthorpe Church, which, like that at Stanley, stands on a hill top, is in the late perpendicular style with a tower at its west end. St James's, in the low-lying area of Thornes, is in a plain Classical style.

Both the increase in the population and the belief that the working classes in particular stood in need of more readily available church provision, led to national and regional moves to build more churches, A meeting in the Court House in Wakefield on 5 September 1838 brought together 'the nobility, gentry and clergy of the West Riding' and resulted in the forming of the Ripon Diocesan Church Building Society. Its secretary was the Reverend John Sharp of Horbury.

Figure 60: St Paul's Church, Alverthorpe. *The author*

Figure 61: St James' Church, Thornes. *Yorkshire Archaeological Society*

This was a period when the Oxford (sometimes known as the Ritualist) Movement, with its desire to recapture something of both the architecture and the ritual of the medieval Catholic church, albeit within the Established Church, was becoming influential. A critical question was whether these new churches should be Anglo-Catholic, reflecting medieval styles, or have the simplicity deemed Evangelical.

The Evangelicals got in first in Wakefield with the building of Holy Trinity Church, in George Street, in 1838-9. The ostensible reason for a third church within the town was the need to provide more accommodation for the growing population and especially for the poor. The 1831 census showed that the town had 12,232 inhabitants. Between them the parish church and St John's Church could hold only 2,700. Most of their pews were privately owned. Neither had many 'free sittings'. The new church was to hold a further 1,000 with one third of the sittings being free. But in this period of tension between people of the low-church persuasion and those influenced by the Oxford Movement, it seems likely that the desire to provide an evangelical approach was uppermost in the minds of the promoters. Robert Hodgson of Haigh Hall gave the land. An advertisement in *The Wakefield Journal* on 2 March 1838 invited subscriptions and listed the promoters. The subscription list was headed by Charles Longley, the first Bishop of Ripon (and later the archbishop of Canterbury) who was notably opposed to Anglo-Catholicism. The vicar of Wakefield, who had Ritualist leanings. and in whose parish the new church was to lie, was not apparently on it. A meeting of subscribers and well-wishers in April 1838 was told that almost £3,000 had already been promised; a committee was established to carry the scheme to fruition. By June the committee was offering ten guineas for the best plans. The foundation stone was laid by the Bishop of Ripon on 9 August. Further funds towards the building costs were raised by a three-day bazaar, planned months in advance, and held in September 1839 in the saloon of the newly opened Corn Exchange. This was very much a ladies' event. Patronesses, rather than patrons, were sought and included more than a dozen titled ladies from across the county. Each of the eight stalls was under the care of two or three of Wakefield's middle-class women. Sixty-four women created a vast carpet of squares worked in Berlin wool and stitched together by Wakefield upholsterer Mrs Hodgson.

The patronage of Holy Trinity was vested in five trustees, the Reverend Jocelyn Willey, then of Cambleforth Hall, The Reverend Oliver Levey Collins, the Reverend Disney Robinson, then vicar of Woolley, and two laymen, John Jones and Henry Lumb. Pews in the new church were advertised for sale in the local paper in the summer of 1840 with prospective purchasers invited to visit it to make their choice. The church was opened on Thursday, 27 August 1840 with two services at which the addresses were given by Hugh Stowell, incumbent of Christ Church, Salford, and Charles G Davies, the incumbent elect of Holy Trinity itself (Figure 62).

Among Holy Trinity's earliest adherents were the family which was to produce

Figure 62: The interior of Holy Trinity Church. *Yorkshire Archaeological Society*

one of the leading hymn-tune composers of the nineteenth century, John Bacchus Dykes (1823-1876) many of whose tunes remain well-known in the twenty-first century. William Dykes came to Wakefield in 1841 as manager of the Wakefield and Barnsley Union Bank. He became honorary choirmaster at Holy Trinity and John, one of his many children, often played the organ. No doubt William Dykes was instrumental in bringing his father, the Reverend Thomas Dykes, from Hull to preach at the time of the church's consecration by the Bishop of Ripon on 30 September 1843. Holy Trinity was designated as a 'particular district' in March 1844. It became a parish, under an Act of Parliament of 1856, only in 1876.

It was people of an Anglo-Catholic disposition who reclaimed the Chantry Chapel on Wakefield Bridge for the Church in the 1840s. There had originally been four free-standing chantries on the perimeter of Wakefield, one on each of the principal routes into the town, but those dedicated to Mary Magdalene (at Westgate End), St John (in Northgate) and St Swithin (near Clarke Hall on the old route to York) had long gone. Despite being in secular hands since the Reformation, and used for many, doubtless inappropriate, purposes, the Wakefield Bridge Chantry had survived, largely because it was important as a buttress to the bridge itself. When the Yorkshire Architectural Society was formed in 1842, amid the enthusiasm among Anglo-Catholics for medieval church architecture, it adopted as one of its objects 'the restoration of mutilated medieval remains'. The Vicar of Wakefield, Samuel Sharp, seized the opportunity, proposing at a meeting of the Society that it restore the Wakefield Chantry. The chapel had been, since the early seventeenth century, in the hands of the Trustees of the Wakefield Poor. In the eighteenth century it was leased by the West Riding magistrates to enable them to keep it, and thus the bridge itself, in some state of repair. Sharp, a trustee of the Wakefield Poor himself, persuaded his colleagues to give the building back to the Church of England free of charge. The Ecclesiastical Commissioners agreed. He then persuaded the magistrates, at Quarter Sessions, to relinquish their lease and to give notice to their tenant. The Yorkshire Architectural Society announced a competition for plans for the chapel's restoration. The winning scheme was that of George Gilbert Scott (1811-1878), who proposed removing all but the medieval crypt and building his idea of a replica of the original chantry. Re-opened in 1848 as a place of worship, the Chantry was by then in the new ecclesiastical district of St Mary's and served as its parish church for six years (Figure 63).

Figure 63: The Chantry Chapel of St Mary the Virgin, Wakefield Bridge. *The author*

The Church Extension Act of 1843 enabled Anglicans, in particular in large and very populous parishes, to build further churches. The Act provided that, where the incumbent and the bishop were satisfied, new ecclesiastical districts could be carved out of the existing parish. Its vicar would receive compensation for the losses he would experience from the income from Easter offerings and fees. A local Act of 1844 created the two districts of St Andrew and St Mary in the south-eastern part of Wakefield. The new incumbent of St Andrew's, the Reverend William Bowditch, swiftly opened a mission room and both a day and Sunday school. The site for the church itself was given by Andrew T T Peterson and St Andrew's Church, fronted onto the newly laid out Peterson Road. St Andrew's, designed by George Gilbert Scott, was completed in 1846. A mission chapel, the 'tin tabernacle' in Pinderfields Road, was dedicated by the first bishop of Wakefield, William Walsham How, on 11 December 1896.

It took rather more time for St Mary's to gain its church. The first incumbent, the Reverend Thomas Browne Parkinson, was a keen follower of the Oxford Movement and in 1851, with little done towards building his church, he went over to Rome and joined a Jesuit order. His successor, the Reverend Joseph Senior, appealed for funds for a church, describing his parish as a populous and poor one, embracing 'Navigation, Mills, Warehouses, Station and Dyeworks'. A local architect, Charles Clapham, was engaged (although the real work was done by his assistant, M O Tarbotton) and the church, at the upper end of Charles Street, was consecrated by the Bishop of Ripon on 29 August 1864. St Mary's mission room, in a former cabinet maker's works in Pincheon Street, was opened in June 1888 in what was described as a 'thickly populated and spiritually needy' area.

St Michael's, created from the parish of Alverthorpe, was, like St Mary's, in a very poor district. It originated as a mission room in Horbury Road in 1856. The church was designed by William Dykes, another son of bank manager William Dykes, who had a practice in York and, at the junction of Dewsbury and Horbury Roads, was on the site of the *Old Swan* public house. Its projected tower never rose, because of shortage of money, above its stump. Although the church opened on 29 September 1858, the lack of money for an endowment meant that it was not consecrated until 27 May 1861 (Figure 64).

St Faith's, on the corner of Eastmoor Road and Stanley Road, was built for the West Riding Pauper Lunatic Asylum and opened on 6 October 1861, replacing an earlier chapel within the Asylum buildings. A twenty-four-strong choir was made up of officers and servants of the hospital. Its design mirrored that for St James's Church, Doncaster, which had been financed primarily by shareholders of the Great Northern Railway. It was not, of course, a parish church and its services were normally taken by the hospital chaplain. It closed in 1996.

St Catherine's began in 1871 as a mission room for St Helen's Church, Sandal, to serve the growing population of Belle Vue, with a Sunday School and regular services. The original plans for the church were for a simple iron mission chapel

Figure 64: St Michael's Church. *Yorkshire Archaeological Society*

but, in the event, a handsome stone church was built, designed in the Early English style by William Watson. Although Belle Vue still lay outside the municipal borough, the foundation stone was laid by the Mayor of Wakefield on 7 April 1872. It was consecrated by the Bishop of Ripon in October 1876 at a time when there was a major housing development (of 200 new homes) in the area.

Under the New Parishes Acts of 1843 and 1856 new districts could be formed with the agreement of the bishop of the diocese and provided that there was an endowment which would yield at least £150 a year. In 1873 Rebecca Disney Robinson, the staunchly Evangelical widow of Reverend Disney Robinson, chose to endow a new church in Thornes Lane, taking a part of the parish of Thornes and a part of the district of Holy Trinity. The impetus for the new, and firmly Evangelical, church came from members of Holy Trinity itself. It was to be called Christ Church and to have room for 600 people with all the sittings free. Mrs Robinson agreed to provide a vicarage as well as an endowment for the church of

£2,400. It was to have schools for 250-300 children and a Mission Room. She was herself to be the patron, ensuring that the incumbents suited her spiritual bent. In all Mrs Disney Robinson contributed £8,700. The church was completed in 1876 and was consecrated in April of the same year. The first incumbent, the Reverend Somerset Edward Pennefather was there only from 1874-5. His successor, the Reverend Alexander Scott, stayed again quite briefly from 1875-1880.

Subscribers to Christ Church schools included Edward Green, then chairman of the Wakefield School Board, and the Unitarian Daniel Gaskell as well as mill-owner Joseph Barker, Benjamin Dixon, the firm of Hodgson and Simpson, and W H B Tomlinson.

The vicarage Mrs Robinson provided was, according to the Reverend James Allan Pride, the incumbent in 1892, built 'in the most shameful manner'. It was close to the street with no difference in level between the pavement and the ground floor of the house. The great flood of 1892 reached a level of two feet in the principal rooms. The roof had been finished with zinc rather than lead and Mr Pride complained that in wet weather he needed buckets in a dozen places to catch the leaks.

Catholicism – Roman and Anglican, and other controversies

Although Roman Catholicism, proscribed at the Reformation, was not formally approved in England until the Catholic Emancipation Act of 1829, a few Catholic chapels were built from 1790 onwards and some families, like the Watertons at Walton Hall, had never given up their Catholic adherence. The first nineteenth-century missioner to Wakefield was the Reverend George Morris who came to the town in 1826. Charles ('Squire') Waterton was energetic in seeking out a site for a church and in 1827 land in Wentworth Terrace was bought from Thomas Rishworth. Catholics felt it necessary to exercise some discretion – anti-Papal riots were still liable to break out – and St Austin's, built by William Puckrin was a humble, plain brick structure with sash windows, little different from the Georgian houses nearby. It was registered at the West Riding Quarter Sessions on 17 January 1828 as 'a papal mass house' and was opened on 4 March. There were thirty in the initial congregation. There were alterations designed by Andrews and Delaney of Bradford in 1852.

Anti-catholic sentiments led to a fiery meeting in the Court House on 1 July 1836 – very possibly engineered by the Evangelical Disney Robinson, when Squire Waterton was present and quick to interrupt the guest speaker. The meeting, to found a branch of the Protestant Reformation Society (protecting the Anglican Church against the Catholic tendencies within it and entirely hostile to the Roman Catholics) had to be terminated and was resumed the following day with a 'ticket-only' audience in the Music Saloon. Neither the Vicar of Wakefield nor the Vicar of St John's attended either meeting. A leading anti-Catholic polemicist, the Reverend Michael Hobart Seymour, spoke at the second meeting of the 'progressive increase of the Church of Rome ... which ought to awaken the most serious apprehension in the minds of Protestants for the spiritual prosperity of the British Dominions'.

Anglo-Catholics favoured the architecture of the medieval church as being God's own style, as distinct from classical architecture which was to be regarded as pagan. John Sharp, the Ritualist incumbent of Horbury church and son of the vicar of Wakefield, lectured, no doubt provocatively, in Wakefield Court House in 1845 on Church Architecture praising the Early English and Perpendicular styles and arguing in the case of the latter that 'the long straight lines rising upward carry the soul onwards to dwell upon the place of the resurrection'. Anglo-Catholics took an interest in plainsong, associated with the medieval Catholic Church, and John Sharp founded a local Plainsong Union. This led to a festival at Stanley Church in June 1875 with choirs from a number of 'high' churches taking part.

William Tait, the incumbent of Holy Trinity Church, preached a series of well-publicised sermons in 1851 on the Errors of Romanism, expressing concern at the current 'growth of Popery'. There were sporadic attacks on the 'Popery' within the Church of England for the remainder of the century, St Michael's and St Peter's at Horbury being the principal targets. In 1867 a letter in *The Wakefield Free Press* complained of 'the genuflexions of the worshippers and the strange antics of the priest' at St Michael's. A year later there was a satirical letter describing a procession of Sunday School boys to 'their Puseyite church', wearing 'things' with tassels on their heads and led by a gentleman in 'strange habiliments'. An editorial a week later explained that Ritualism was to be deplored as it was the path 'to the Vatican'. In 1869 an editorial in *The Wakefield Express* spoke of the people of Horbury 'who have long borne the Romish practices carried out by the Reverend John Sharp' being ready to take a determined stand against them. It criticised the form of worship and the furnishings of the church and mocked the three curates who 'go about habited in the dress of French Roman Catholic cures'.

The vicar of St Andrew's, William Bowditch, gave an apparently quite fiery lecture in the Music Saloon in April 1867 attacking the principle of religious dissent. The question was one of where 'authority' lay. Nonconformists, he argued, believed that the individual should be independent of any spiritual authority whereas the Established Church properly accepted the authority inherited from the apostles. On this ground, interference with the spiritual lives of others was right.

On the whole the different factions in Wakefield lived together peaceably, making their views heard at meetings or in the columns of the local press rather than by taking to the streets. But the more hot-headed elements, or those who felt threatened, could be stirred to riot by a rabble-rouser. When the French anti-Catholic speaker who styled himself Baron de Camin came to Wakefield in October 1856, a crowd of Irish people awaited him in Wood Street. However he was denied access to the Music Saloon to give his talk and, for the time, his Wakefield campaign ended without incident. His return in August 1862, led to a good deal of brick-throwing and window-breaking. De Camin again had difficulty in obtaining anywhere to give his vitriolic lecture and, after being refused access to the Music Saloon, the Corn Exchange and the theatre, he spoke to a crowded Wood Street from a balcony at the *Royal Hotel* (formerly the *Woodman*). The Irish were there in force. Camin's stock-in-trade was to vilify Catholic convents as brothels where, he said, there were men dressed up as nuns as well as women, to denounce the Catholic Church as a political association for enslaving people, and to insist that the Pope intended the conquest of England. The subsequent rioting took place primarily in the Irish areas of New Street and Providence Street, in Westgate, where the *Saddle Inn*, which had an Irish landlord, was attacked. and in Brooksbank and Salt Pie Alley where, again, there were Irish residents. It took the Wakefield police, members of the County force and special constables sworn in for the purpose, to achieve order.

It is likely that the real issue behind the violence was whether or not orators could have freedom to speak rather than whether Popery was a threat.

Mrs Disney Robinson was so strongly opposed to ritualism that in the 1880s she bought the advowsons (the right to appoint vicars) of St Andrew's, St Mary's and Sandal churches to ensure that they would always have low-church incumbents. Since that time the advowsons have been held, according to Mrs Robinson's wishes, by the Peache Trustees.

William Bowditch, the long-serving first vicar of St Andrew's, was a Ritualist. In 1885, when Arthur Whaley succeeded him, one local paper remarked that, 'During the late vicar's time, the services were conducted with all the rites and ceremonies of the ritualistic portion of the Church of England, but henceforth there will be a new order of things and Mr Whaley will conduct the services of his church according to the views of the evangelical party.' There would be no more candlesticks and no more turning to the east for the Creed.

There was some controversy in 1866 when there was a national cattle plague. A number of citizens called on the Mayor to declare a Day of Humiliation on 14 March 1866. There were services and sermons at the Anglican and Methodist churches and at Zion. However there was an article in *The Wakefield Free Press* arguing that 'physical disease among cattle cannot be a legitimate cause' for such an event. The Reverend Goodwyn Barmby, Unitarian minister at Westgate Chapel, argued that the cattle plague was not a punishment from God but a result of human failure in looking after the livestock.

Missionary activities
Nonconformists and Anglicans alike were concerned both at the absence of the working classes from places of worship and at their intemperate habits.

The Wakefield Temperance Society was founded in 1835. When a Temperance

Hotel and Coffee House was opened in Westgate two years later, the Society established a newsroom there in an effort to draw people away from public houses where the availability of newspapers was an attraction. The Society opened a new room in Queen Street in February 1860. The pursuit of temperance led to the founding by philanthropists in Wakefield (as elsewhere) of cocoa and coffee taverns where working men could enjoy almost all the amenities of a public house other than intoxicating drink. They were normally run as companies but the dividends to shareholders were small. The first of those in Wakefield, the *Market Tavern*, was opened on 16 August 1878 by the High Sheriff of Yorkshire, William Aldam. A large mug of coffee or cocoa cost 1d. Tea was rather dearer at 2d. There were pies, scones, ham sandwiches and buns. Tobacco and cigars 'of the best quality' were also available.

Parents of children attending the Ragged School in 1867 were encouraged to 'sign the pledge'.

The Town Mission, founded in 1840, employed 'agents' whose tasks were to conduct services, visit the working classes to read from the scriptures and to distribute tracts, to comfort the sick and to attend the dying. Women were enlisted in 1841-2 to raise funds to give to the destitute. The Mission was dependent on subscriptions, donations, legacies, and collections at special services held, primarily, at the Baptist, Independent and Methodist chapels. In fact the surplus money from the Wakefield fund for the victims of the 1852 disaster, when the Bilberry Reservoir at Holmfirth burst, came to the Mission. The agents held regular services at the Workhouse and, it was reported, saved the Poor Law Union the cost of employing a chaplain.

The Young Men's Christian Association was founded in 1844 by George Williams, a draper's assistant in London. The movement spread quite rapidly to the provinces, including Leeds, but it was not until 7 October 1875 that the Wakefield YMCA was established. In its early years it met in premises in Wood Street opposite the Music Saloon and belonging, it seems to the Mechanics' Institution. It moved to Grove House, Grove Road before Mrs Disney Robinson gave it a building in Red Lion Yard, Kirkgate.

There was increasing concern in the latter part of the century at the absence of the working-class from places of worship. During the 1870s and 1880s there were a number of large-scale missions in Wakefield under the Church of England umbrella. Clergymen with a proven talent for communicating with the lower classes were invited to the town for campaigns of two-weeks or so. They held services in work places and, for example, in 1875 at Kirkgate Station where they were joined by the Town Missionaries. Among other experiments to try to 'bring them in' was a series of Sunday afternoon services held in the Georgian theatre. These took place between 23 December 1888 and May 1889. The group behind the scheme was the Mission Band of the West Parade Christian Workers' Association. Newspaper reports suggest that as many as 700-800 people attended on occasions. The events were described as 'homely' with some of Sankey's hymns and solo renderings of popular items like The Lost Chord.

In the autumn of 1891 there was a series of discussions, at which a good many working men seem to have been present, exploring why men (in particular) did not attend places of worship. Men, it was said, laboured hard and were left with no appetite for spiritual things; they were affronted by the pew-ownership or pew-rent system; the clergy were too dictatorial and their preaching was too theological; they did nothing for working men. The Christian Church was too divided.

Societies concerned with the spreading of religion amongst the 'heathen' in other parts of the world were founded from the early part of the nineteenth century. The Wakefield Bible Society was formed c1814. The Wakefield branch of the (Anglican) Church Missionary Society followed in March 1820.

1814 saw a Society formed in Wakefield for the Abolition of Slavery, bringing together Anglicans, Quakers, Unitarians and others. In 1830 there was a public meeting called by the Constable to petition Parliament again on the issue of slavery. There was a renewal of interest leading to the formation, again on an interdenominational basis, of the Wakefield Anti-Slavery Society on 12 January 1860.

Resisting the church rate

The obligation for all householders to pay rates for the maintenance of the Established Church was a source of contention nationally among Nonconformists and some churchmen. The rate was set by the churchwardens and came before an annual Vestry meeting for approval.

At the beginning of the century, the Wakefield rate supported the upkeep of the parish church and St John's Church. The building of Alverthorpe, Stanley and Thornes Churches added substantially to the rate. Some Wakefield Radicals, including George Craven and Joseph Horner, refused to pay the supplementary church rate levied in 1831.

In 1836 Craven, who had served as the Constable of Wakefield in 1832 and 1833, took the issue to the Assizes in York. He argued that the church rate was illegal since, although Horbury Church was a chapel-of-ease, like those at Alverthorpe, Stanley, and Thornes, no rate was levied by the Wakefield churchwardens on the people of Horbury. The defendants argued successfully that Horbury church had always been maintained independently, principally by the Horbury Common Lands Trust but, as and when needed, by an occasional local rate.

In 1837 a bill was brought before Parliament for the abolition of Church Rates. Petitions were drawn up in Wakefield both for and against the bill. The radical one, opposing the Church Rate, was very possibly devised by Martin Naylor. At the request of 114 signatories, the Constable, George Green, called a public meeting in the Court House in April where feelings ran high but which resulted in agreement to forward the petition supporting abolition. A further petition was sent by pupils at the Nonconformist Lancasterian School and at the Congregational school at Silcoates. The Head of the Proprietory School forbade boys to sign. The bill failed. In 1845 George W Harrison, leading the opposition to the rate at the time, made the 'Romish tendencies' at the parish church one of the grounds of objection. A poll of all ratepayers was demanded and took place over a fortnight amidst noisy scenes and the swearing in of special constables. The objectors were in the majority until the last days but finally the pro-rate church party won by fifteen votes.

The renewal of places of worship

The 1860s, 70s and 80s saw the renewal and rebuilding of many of Wakefield's places of worship. In 1860 the parish church spire and the upper part of the tower were taken down and rebuilt, members of the public enjoying the chance to climb the scaffolding. Further considerable alterations were completed in 1874. Holy Trinity was enlarged in 1868 and a new vestry added in 1891. The Wesleyan Chapel at Eastmoor was replaced by a new building opened in May 1871 and the old building was sold. The Baptist Chapel was extended in 1876 to designs by Mr Lynam. The organ was removed from the gallery to an apse which was built behind the pulpit and several classrooms were added at the rear. St Austin's Roman Catholic Church in Wentworth Terrace was radically altered in 1878-9 to the designs of Joseph Hansom (of Hansom cab fame). At the same time, Huddersfield architects John Kirk and sons were engaged to oversee ambitious alterations to Ebenezer Primitive Methodist Chapel. The floor was raised by four and a half feet, using jacks, giving considerably more height to the basement. The gallery was removed and the chapel was lengthened by six feet; a minister's vestry was added at

Figure 65: The new front of Ebenezer Primitive Methodist Chapel of 1880. *The author*

the back of the chapel in Queen Street and a wholly new front was built in Market Street (Figure 65). West Parade Wesleyan Methodist Chapel saw alterations in 1880 with new pews, a remodelled pulpit and the addition of minister's and choir vestries. There were radical alterations to the interior layout of the Unitarian Westgate Chapel in the early 1880s: the original box pews were replaced by 'modern' walnut pews and a vestry was added at the rear. The ends of the box pews were used to form a dado. In 1886-7 Thornes Church was extensively modernised at the expense of the industrialist Joseph Barker. It was re-floored with pitch-pine blocks, oak stalls were put in for the choir, a new heating system was installed, and the chairs which had formerly been in tiers were placed on one level all facing east. St Catherine's gained a new vestry and organ chamber in 1890.

A major anniversary

The centenary of the founding of the first Sunday School by Robert Raikes (1736-1811) was celebrated in July 1880 by almost all the denominations in Wakefield with segregation between the Anglicans and the Nonconformists, some grumbling, and, generally speaking, much good will. People argued that all religious groups should have come together for a single massive celebration. Nonconformists leaders said that they had understood that some teachers in the Established Church schools had preferred to have a separate event. The Unitarians were, despite a last-minute invitation to join the other Nonconformists, left out, primarily, the Nonconformist leaders said, out of consideration for their tender feelings when hymns had been chosen that would be alien to their theology. The Anglicans probably had the better party, meeting on the Grammar School playing fields and enjoying a firework display. The Nonconformists met in the yard of the Rifle Volunteers Drill Hall for hymns and speeches.

Wakefield hosts the national Church Congress

The greatest gathering of church people ever held in Wakefield was the Church Congress in October 1886. The annual Congress had been founded in 1861 when, on a modest scale, it took place in Cambridge. It was a voluntary gathering, bringing together Anglican clergy from archbishops to curates, together with lay people, and embracing evangelicals, ritualists and the broad church party. Wakefield seems to have been chosen because it was shortly to become the cathedral city of a new diocese. Every major building in the centre of Wakefield was in use. The trade floor of the Corn Exchange was converted into the Congress Hall with the erection of a platform that could hold 200 and galleries on the other three sides. The assembly room above it became the Sectional Hall for smaller gatherings. New doors were opened on the east and west sides towards the southern end of the building. The offices of the Wakefield Charities became the press room and the Wakefield postmaster, William Pye, ensured that reports could be sent by electric telegraph to all parts of Britain.

Nonconformist chapels lent their premises for 'fringe' meetings. The Music Saloon, the hall of the Church Institute, and the schoolrooms at West Parade Methodist Chapel and Holy Trinity Church were taken over by local caterers for those who chose not to eat at public houses or inns. There were papers, followed by discussion, on, for example, church and state, the relationship between the church and the rural population, the relationship between the church and the urban population, Religious Education, and visiting the working class in their homes. Fringe meetings included one seeking support for opposing the legalising of marriage with one's deceased wife's sister, one (for men only) on sexual purity, and one promoting the Church of England Funeral and Mourning Reform Association. One of the country's leading clerical outfitters exhibited his garments in the Industrial Co-operative Society's store in Bank Street. Grace's fine art gallery in Westgate exhibited Sir Noel Paton's painting, Watch and Pray. The Congress opened on Tuesday, 5 October with a reception at the Town Hall for the leading speakers, organisers and attending clergy, followed by processions to the parish church, St John's and Holy Trinity where services took place simultaneously.

Wakefield becomes a Diocese

Wakefield became a city in 1888 when the diocese of Wakefield was created and the parish church elevated to cathedral status (Figure 66). The new diocese had been a long time coming. Between the sixteenth and nineteenth centuries, no new bishoprics had been established. Then came the dioceses of Ripon (1836), and Manchester (1845). By 1875 the population of the Ripon diocese had doubled, from 800,000 at its inception to 1,600,000. In 1875 there were moves to create a further bishopric in Yorkshire with Halifax as its cathedral city. These came to nothing but the Government set up a committee to look at the need nationally for new bishoprics. Its initial recommendations were for sees centred on Liverpool, Newcastle and Southwell. When the first bill was drafted in 1877 a diocese of South Yorkshire had been added which would have included Sheffield (not part of the diocese of Ripon) as well as Halifax and Wakefield and places between. The prospect of being severed from York did not appeal to the churchpeople of Sheffield and when the bill came before Parliament Sheffield had been dropped from it. There was a public meeting in Wakefield on 23 May 1877 to seek formal

Figure 66: Wakefield Cathedral.
The author

support for the 'superior' claims of the town. Substantial sums of money were required and a number of Wakefield people made individual donations of £1000. When the new Bishop of Ripon, Dr Boyd Carpenter, paid his first visit to Wakefield in 1885 to attend a Church Institution soiree, Wakefield's then vicar, Canon Norman Straton and the erstwhile MP Robert Mackie urged him to exercise his good offices to secure the swift division of his diocese. Wakefield's first bishop was William Walsham How (1823-1897) who had spent twenty-eight years as Rector of Whittington, Shropshire, before, styled Bishop of Bedford, becoming a suffragan to the Bishop of London in 1879 (Figure 67). How was, for a new diocese, primarily a safe pair of hands. He was of high-church leanings but was not a Tractarian: he conducted retreats and held quiet days, but he abhorred some of the ritual associated with the Oxford Movement. When he first came to Wakefield, he lived at Thornhill Rectory. He moved to a house in South Parade, Wakefield, and then to Overthorpe Hall, Thornhill. The foundation stone of the bishop's new house, Bishopgarth in Westfield Road, was laid in October

Figure 67: William Walsham How, first bishop of Wakefield. *Wakefield Historical Publications*

1891 by Mrs Boyd Carpenter, wife of the Bishop of Ripon (Figure 68). How was a strong supporter of Wakefield's Technical and Art College and the Grammar and High Schools. A keen fly-fisher and botanist, he supported the Wakefield Paxton Society. His major legacy to Wakefield was the Bede Home for Boys, in

Figure 68: Bishopgarth. *The John Goodchild Collection*

College Grove Road. He had been instrumental in the decision of the Church of England Society for Providing Homes for Waifs and Strays to build a home in Wakefield. It was formally opened in 1892. It closed in 1967 and the house was redeveloped as flats. How is perhaps best known today as a hymn writer, in particular as the author of For all the Saints, that from their labours rest. Less well known is the consternation he stirred when, responding to a leading article in *The Yorkshire Post*, which had roundly comdemned the novelist Thomas Hardy, he wrote to the paper in June 1896 claiming to have been so 'disgusted with its insolence and indecency' that he threw *Jude the Obscure* on the fire.

Sources

R H Malden, *A Short History of the Diocese of Ripon: 1836-1936*, 1936.

Benjamin Rayson, 'A letter to the congregation at Salem Chapel', included in a volume of sermons of 1823.

Samuel Horner, manuscript letter of 1849, in the John Goodchild Collection.

John Goodchild, unpublished history of Salem Chapel.

Paul Dawson, 'The History of West Parade Methodist Chapel', *Aspects of Wakefield 2*, 1999.

Richard Cope, *The Autobiography of the Reverend Richard Cope LL.D, edited by his son*, 1857.

Author unknown, manuscript transcript of talk given at the opening of a bazaar to raise funds for paying off the mortgage on Bethel Chapel, The John Goodchild Collection.

John Goodchild, unpublished talk on Flanshaw Chapel.

Derek Linstrum, *West Yorkshire Architects and Architecture*, 1978.

J T Fowler, ed, *Life and Letters of the Rev. John Bacchus Dykes*, 1897.

Kate Taylor, *This Pious Undertaking*, 2003.

Papers held at the Church of England Record Centre relating to Christ Church and Holy Trinity Church.

Reports of the Wakefield Town Mission.

Geoffrey T Willett, *New Parishes Grow Old: St Andrew and St Mary*, 1974.

John Goodchild, *What's Where at Westgate*, 1996.

Norman D Straton, *The Wakefield Bishopric Movement*, 1888.

5   *E*DUCATION

However desirable it might seem to the modern mind, there was no legal requirement for any children to have a formal education until 1833 and then the only provision, under the Factory Act, was for children who worked in factories to attend school for a minimum of two hours a day on six days a week. Compulsory education for all came only in the 1870s. Until then the only state support was via grants towards the building costs of voluntary schools from 1833, and to qualified teachers, apprentice teachers and their mentors from 1846. Voluntary schools earned grants for the achievements of individual pupils on the basis of satisfactory attendance from 1853, and on the basis of both attendance and attainment (primarily in the three Rs) from 1862.

In 1801 Wakefield children who had a formal education gained it through either privilege or charity.

Provision for education in Wakefield, as elsewhere, grew in the nineteenth century as a result of local initiatives – including private enterprise, the increasing involvement of religious denominations and the proliferation of their churches and chapels, and in response to national legislation. The need for numerate, literate and technically competent workpeople, such as clerks, bookkeepers and draughtsmen, prompted the development of facilities for adult education.

Figure 69: An inscription on the sixteenth century Grammar School in the Goody Bower. *Yorkshire Archaeological Society*

A number of schools still operating in Wakefield in the twenty-first century, and Wakefield College, trace their history to these nineteenth century developments.

At the beginning of the century, Wakefield had, apart from small private schools, and its Sunday Schools, only the long-established, boys-only Queen Elizabeth Grammar School, in its original premises in Brook Street, and the Green Coat School, administered by the same body of trustees, the Governors of the Wakefield Charities (also known as the Trustees of Wakefield Poor), with premises in Westgate, catering for children of both sexes (Figure 69).

Outside Wakefield itself there were township schools at Alverthorpe and Thornes. Sandal Endowed School, founded under the will of one Richard Taylor of 1686, had had premises since 1747 on the site it still occupies.

The schools administered by the Governors of the Wakefield Charities
The Grammar School was, according to its historian Ronald Chapman, in 1800 'in fearful decline'. Such education as it provided, free of charge, was largely governed by its statutes of 1606 and focused on Latin, Greek, and the principles of the Christian religion. From 1758 it had had a 'writing master' who taught both writing and arithmetic (for which he was able to negotiate a fee) and a year later a special Writing School was added on the north of the main building. French masters were engaged from time to time from 1752. In the early years of the nineteenth century, no formal register was maintained so that it is unclear how many pupils there were but a retrospective roll devised from the memory of the Master and Usher in 1829 suggests that possibly eighty pupils entered the school between 1817 and 1821, or some twenty a year.

The duties of the Master were clearly by no means full time. The Reverend Dr Martin Naylor (1764-1863) was appointed to the position in 1814, remaining there until 1837, assisted by an usher. Naylor had advertised in July 1801 that he boarded and educated a 'limited number' of young gentlemen, preparing them for University, the 'liberal professions' or commercial life. In addition to his position at the school, he edited the Wakefield newspaper, *The Wakefield Journal*, was chaplain at the West Riding Pauper Lunatic Asylum, and held the living of Penistone – generally *in absentia*. He was also president of Wakefield Museum, a probably short-lived enterprise of the 1820s-30s, founded by the Wakefield Literary and Philosophical Society and providing for subscribers in a room in Northgate. Naylor's daughters opened a school in the family home in Sandal in 1820 advertising that Dr Naylor would himself supervise the teaching of Grammar and Geography.

A handbill dated 21 January 1820 shows that the hours of attendance at the Grammar School then depended on the time of year: in the spring and summer months attendance was from 8am to 12 noon and 2pm to 6pm. In winter it was from 9am to 12 noon and 2pm to 5pm closing on dark nights, rather earlier. Boys from Wakefield township were taught Latin and Greek free. For anything beyond that, fees were charged. In 1842, for example, the additional subjects, taught by

Figure 70: The West Riding Proprietory School building, acquired in 1854 by the Governors of the Wakefield Charities for the Queen Elizabeth Grammar School. *Yorkshire Archaeological Society*

the master of the Writing School, of Writing, Arithmetic, English, and Geography came at a cost of 10s 6d a quarter for the 'free' scholars and at £1 1s a quarter for others.

The need for a more up-to-date education than grammar schools provided, especially for middle-class boys, led to the founding of the West Riding Proprietory School with purpose-built premises in Northgate, in the 1830s (Figure 70). The project was initiated in 1832 by a group of men from Wakefield and beyond who were 'anxious to secure for their sons a sound liberal education at a cheap rate'. Shares were offered at £25 each. The trustees, acting on behalf of the subscribers, engaged a Manchester architect, Richard Lane who had already designed the town halls at Salford and Chorlton cum Medlock. The foundation stone was laid by the Earl of Mexborough on 6 February 1833 and the school opened in August 1834. Its headmaster was the Reverend G A Butterton. The curriculum included Mathematics, Science and Modern Languages. Boys came from a distance – some from as far away as London – and local householders, and some of the masters themselves, took in boarders. Among pupils at the school in the early 1840s was John Bacchus Dykes, the son of a Wakefield bank manager, who went on to become one of the most prolific writers of (quite splendid) hymn tunes that Britain has ever known. The fees were £10 a year for tuition and a further £35 for boarding.

The Proprietory School survived for less than twenty years. In December 1854 the Northgate premises were offered for sale by auction. This clearly seemed to the headmaster of the Queen Elizabeth Grammar School at the time, the Reverend James Taylor, and his governors far too good an opportunity to miss. Taylor had already complained in 1848 that the school was 'surrounded by slaughter houses, dung heaps and the most disreputable and offensive lanes and alleys of the town'. 'Owing to the prevalence of cholera all round, the medical men of the district ordered the school to be closed,' he said, 'But though the cholera added a new objection to the situation of the school, it was a small one compared with the physical and moral nuisances of a permanent character'. There were plans subsequently to build a new school at Cliff Hill and subscribers offered £700 of the £1000 required. The opening of the Borough Market in 1851 added very substantially to the obnoxious nature of the vicinity of the school. But then came the golden opportunity. The spokesman of the Governors, the Reverend and Honourable Philip Yorke Savile, was present in person at the auction to make the winning bid of £4,500. Some of this was recompensed when shareholders in the Proprietory School gave their holdings to the Governors. The school moved to Northgate the following year.

The curriculum of the Grammar School was then drastically revised and whilst there was emphasis still on Religious Instruction in the principles of the Church of England, it now included French, Algebra, Arithmetic, Geography, Ancient and Modern History and English Literature. German, Drawing and Music could also be taught at the instigation of the Head Master and with the consent of the Governors. In fact John Battye Tootal, who had taught at the Proprietory School, was engaged as a drawing master in 1855. Scientific subjects were notably absent. Science was, however, added in 1875 under a new scheme drawn up by the Charity Commission at a time when the school had a mere twenty-six pupils. The Reverend James Taylor, who was 'a writer of pamphlets', left and for the first time a layman was appointed as the headmaster. The Charity Commission scheme insisted that no headmaster should 'hold any benefice involving the cure of souls or any other appointment which would interfere with the proper execution of his duties'. Another step towards modernity lay in the provision for the Mayor of Wakefield and the chairman of the School Board to be governors.

The Grammar School acquired additional facilities in 1893, marking the 300 anniversary of its foundation. A new block, opened on 28 October, included a Science lecture room, an Art room, a Chemistry Laboratory and a gymnasium. The laying of the foundation stone in November 1891 was marked with a service in Wakefield Cathedral and a dinner in the Town Hall.

In 2008 the Grammar School remains in the Proprietory School premises albeit with a much extended range of buildings.

There was by the 1870s considerable pressure for girls to have similar opportunities for secondary education to boys. The Charity Commission scheme of 1875 provided for the establishing of a girls' school. Wakefield Girls' High

Figure 71: Wakefield Girls' High School. *The author*

School was opened in 1878, by the Governors of the Wakefield Charities, in Wentworth House, a Georgian mansion in Wentworth Street built at the beginning of the nineteenth century for John Pemberton Heywood (Figure 71). The school provided for 'young ladies' aged eight to eighteen. There were differences: there was strong opposition to girls taking part in games, and science, too, was considered unsuitable. Girls had the alternative of taking Needlework. However, Hockey was introduced in 1893 and classes in Science commenced in 1894. The Fives Court was built in 1899. A chemistry laboratory was added in 1905. But even in 1918, when Norah Mulligan began her thirty-year stint teaching Chemistry, science was held in lowly place.

The Green Coat School, which provided elementary education, had originated from two sources – the Storie Pettie Gift of 1674, provided under the will of John Storie, which was administered by the Governors of the Wakefield Charities, and the decision of the Governors some time before 1703 to open a charity school under the Elizabethan Poor Law. In 1705 a purpose-built school was opened in Westgate, a little lower down than the junction with what is now Drury Lane. Income came from a variety of sources including rents from users of the Market Cross and from the Cattle Market. From time to time funds were raised by the preaching of sermons and an offertory at St John's and Wakefield parish churches. Until 1831 children attended free of charge and numbers of them were also clothed, in the distinctive uniform which gave the school its name. However, after money was required for alterations at the Cattle Market, pupils were charged 1d a week. In 1811 the girls were moved to premises in Pincheon Street and from there to Almshouse Lane. When Sir Joshua Girling Fitch of the Taunton Commission visited the school in the 1860s, he reported that there were 140 boys and 70 girls on its roll. After the Grammar School moved to Northgate, the Green Coat School took over its vacated premises in Brook Street, for the boys, in 1857. In 1860 John William Young came as Master to the Green Coat School from St Mary's National School. From then until the school's closure, the parish church choir was drawn from its boys. Ironically, when the Green Coat school was flourishing under Young, the moves towards its closure began. In 1866 five Wakefield clergy complained to the Governors of the Wakefield Charities that their parish National Schools were suffering from the unfair competition: because of its endowments, Green Coat children paid only 1d a week, whilst the parish schools had to charge 3d or 4d a week. Children trying to obtain places at the charity school left their own schools, missing the vital examinations and depriving the parish schools of the associated government funding. Moreover, the charity children enjoyed the opportunities for apprenticeship provided under the 1722 will of a Wakefield maltster, John Bromley which brought in some £700 a year for that purpose. As many as 100 boys might be in apprenticeships at a time. The sources of grievance were addressed by Fitch who was by then the Inspector of Schools of the West Riding on behalf of the School Inquiry Commission. The school closed in 1875. The income from the Storie gift was then applied to provide twenty-four scholarships at the Grammar School and twelve at the Girls' High School.

In 1877 the premises that had housed the Green Coat girls in Almshouse Lane were in use for what the directory labelled a 'middle-class' school.

Silcoates, still flourishing as an independent school, was founded in Silcoates Hall in 1820 as a grammar school for dissenters. It was refounded in 1832 as the Northern Congregational School primarily as a boarding school for the sons of ministers whose fees were subsidised by subscriptions. Its high reputation drew other scholars. In 1868, at the time of the Inquiry Commission, the fees for ministers' sons were £15 a year whilst thirty other boys were educated at £30 a year. In 1873 it gained impressive purpose-designed buildings.

Sunday Schools
It had been accepted since the 1780s that basic education could be taught on Sundays. Robert Raikes, whose name is linked with the Sunday School movement, opened his school in Gloucester in that year. Prayers and hymns were certainly a part, but perhaps not all, of the curriculum. Wakefield's first Sunday School was opened in the cellar of the *Great Bull Hotel* in Westgate in November 1784. Among its benefactors was Sir Michael Pilkington, with a grant of £50. In honour of the event, and the 480 scholars said to have enrolled, the Wakefield Society of Ringers spent three hours and twenty-five minutes providing a peal named Union Bob Tripples on 28 November. The children arrived at 8am for two hours' schooling before being accompanied by their teachers to the parish

church. They returned to the classroom at 2pm and remained there until 6pm. Civilising the working classes seems at that time to have been a more important influence than the necessity to have an educated work force. *The Leeds Mercury* observed that 'the establishing of Sunday Schools in so many towns and villages is a pleasing proof that the public at large is convinced of the absolute necessity of a reformation of manners'. By 1811 there were 1,171 pupils on the roll being taught in eleven different places in the city centre.

Early in the nineteenth century Sunday Schools were established by the Nonconformist denominations and, as more Anglican churches were built, each of them had its Sunday school too. An extensive survey for *The Leeds Mercury* in 1843 showed the Wakefield township as having two church Sunday Schools and fourteen run by other denominations. The 1851 Education Census, which included the townships of Alverthorpe with Thornes and Stanley cum Wrenthorpe in the Wakefield figures, recorded that on 30 March there were 4,000 children on the rolls of sixty-two Sunday Schools (although only 2,161 actually attended on that day).

The first elementary schools
The first new day schools – rival foundations – came in 1812 and 1813. The earlier, the Lancasterian School, on the corner of Newstead Road and Margaret Street, was explicitly undenominational. The Bell School, built close by, and from which Bell Street takes its name, was under the control of members of the established church. (Figure 72). Church of England elementary schools became known throughout the country as National schools.

The initial meeting which led to the foundation of the Lancasterian School was held in the Sunday School at Salem Chapel on 2 March 1812. This was followed on 11 March by a public meeting at the *Woolpacks Hotel* for people of every denomination. There was evidently a desire to draw the Established Church as well as Dissenters into the scheme and further action was postponed until 25 March to give the Anglicans a chance to participate. At that meeting, chaired by the Unitarian John Pemberton Heywood, it was agreed that children of all denominations should be admitted to the school and that they should remain free to attend whatever place of worship they (or their parents) chose. A committee was to be formed with equal numbers of representatives from every church or chapel. All clergy and ministers regularly officiating in Wakefield were to be permanent members of the committee.

Any hope of cooperation from the Established Church was quickly extinguished. Just a week later there was an 'establishment' meeting, convened by the Constable of Wakefield and held in the vestry of the parish church, which resolved to set up a society for promoting the education of the poor in 'suitable learning' and 'the principles of the Christian religion according to the Established Church'. The committee included the clergy and and some townspeople from the parish of Wakefield together with the vicars of Sandal and of Warmfield. It was

Figure 72: The Bell School. *Yorkshire Archaeological Society*

Figure 73: A drawing of the Elizabethan Grammar School in the 1880s by Henry Clarke. *Wakefield Historical Society*

agreed that no child should be excluded simply because its parents were Dissenters. The school was to cater for children between the ages of five and thirteen.

Initially both schools catered only for boys but the Anglicans soon provided a school for girls, in Almshouse Lane, and the Nonconformists accepted girls from 1814. Both the Lancasterian and Bell schools worked on the monitorial system, where older pupils – the monitors – taught the younger ones. The system had been pioneered by an Anglican minister, the Reverend Andrew Bell, who introduced it at St Botolph's School, London, in 1798, and a Quaker, Joseph Lancaster, who had founded a school in Borough Road, London, in 1803. The Bell School, which moved to Zetland Street, evolved as the parish-church school and, subsequently as the Cathedral School, and is the antecedent of the school still in existence in the twenty-first century. The boys from there moved to the Elizabethan Grammar School building in 1895 (Figure 73). Despite a number of earlier financial crises, the Lancasterian School survived until 1901.

The sectarian impact on education nationally, has continued ever since.

Friction between Nonconformity and the Established Church surfaced in 1843 when it seemed that the Education clauses in the Factory Bill would favour the National Schools. A public meeting was requested with the aim of petitioning Parliament against the bill. The attendance, scathingly described in the Tory *Wakefield Journal*, consisted of an 'unholy alliance of papistical bigotry, unitarian unbelief, and atheistical affrontary'. There were three main criticisms of the bill: it would render manufacturing uneconomic because, having to employ twice as many children in order to allow them time to attend school, they would be unable to compete with businesses on the continent; children would be taught in National schools; education would be compulsory instead of voluntary; the new schools would be subsided from the Poor Rate which was intended for other purposes.

The development of Church of England (National) schools
The Ripon Diocesan Board of Education was founded at a meeting in Wakefield on 2 December 1841 with the aims of 'promoting and improving and extending popular education according to the principles of the Established Church'.

It was expected that elementary schools would be rapidly established in the new ecclesiastical districts founded under the 1843 Church Extension Act. The Act reflected, in part, the belief that the religious and moral teaching provided by the National schools was a vital means of 'civilising' the working-classes. Both the new districts of St Mary's and St Andrew's opened day schools in the 1840s. St Andrew's was built on Green Hill Road on a site acquired from the Governors of the Wakefield Charities. The school was known locally simply as 'Mr Bowditch's'. The Reverend William Bowditch, the first incumbent, clearly intended to manage it himself but the Government's Committee in Council

insisted that a management committee be formed to include the churchwardens
and two or three others, each of whom must subscribe at least twenty shillings
a year to the school, who were to be elected by those of their fellow subscribers
who contributed at least ten shillings a year. Bowditch, clearly had aspirations
for his school. Although the infants were all taught together, the older children
were, initially, separated and Bowditch aimed at a curriculum sophisticated for
its day for his boys. He advertised for twenty sons of shopkeepers, tradesmen,
farmers etc. They were to be taught Algebra, Arithmetic, Book-keeping,
Drawing, Geography, Geometry, Grammar and English Language, History,
Mechanics, Mensuration, Music (vocal), Natural History, Reading and Writing.
At the same time he advertised for three pupil teachers aged between thirteen
and sixteen. By 1851 it seems that St Andrew's had an Industrial Farm to teach
practical agriculture to the pupils but little is so far known about the enterprise.
In July 1849, as 'Female Education for the Middle Classes' Bowditch advertised
the opening of St Andrew's Girls' School 'for the daughters of tradesmen.
farmers and others' at six shillings for the first quarter and ten shillings a
quarter thereafter, payable in advance. Other schools in Wakefield were
charging 1d or 2d a week. But again the school proposed a curriculum well
above that of the other local elementary schools, including not only Arithmetic,
Reading, Writing, Spelling and Religious Instruction, but Domestic Economy,
Drawing, Geography (including Physics and the use of globes), Grammar and
the English Language, History, Knitting, Music, Natural History and Sewing
(including the art of cutting out)'. Bowditch later advertised the school in terms
unfamiliar at the time as a 'Middle School'. For a time in 1859 the schools had
to close for lack of funds. Attendance in the 1860s was patchy. Children might
remain at home simply because the weather was wet. They were either given, or
took, days off to attend Wakefield fair and other passing attractions.

Some evidence for the payment of elementary school teachers comes from the
testimony of Elizabeth Gill who taught at St Andrew's School from 1864-1868.
She received the 'school pence', i.e. the weekly payment made by the children,
and had free tenancy of the school house. She was allowed fifteen shillings a
quarter to ensure that the school room was swept and cleaned. Another teacher
at the same school (but not at the same time presumably) was allowed £20 a year
and the tenancy of one of the school houses. The salary was to be taken from the
school pence. Any surplus had to be handed over to the vicar. If there was
underpayment, the vicar was to make up the sum.

The further Church of England schools founded in the Wakefield area
included Holy Trinity, which opened in 1847 with 100 boys and 70 girls on its
roll, Alverthorpe (1848), St James's, Thornes (1851), St Michael's (1851), St
John's (1861) and Christ Church, Thornes Lane, which was built in 1874 largely
at the expense of the evangelical benefactor of the church itself, Mrs Disney
Robinson.

Figure 74: The Methodist School in Thornhill Street. *Simon Jenkins*

Nonconformist and non-sectarian schools

Wakefield's only Methodist school, still flourishing in the twenty-first century although now in premises in Field Lane, Thornes, was opened in July 1846 (Figure 74). The central issue in Education for much of the nineteenth century was not what should be provided in the curriculum but who the providers should be. At their national conference in 1843, the Methodists adopted a resolution that they should build 700 day schools in the next seven years. On 21 December of the same year a meeting at West Parade Chapel approved conference's decision and set up a committee to raise funds locally. A trust was established the following year. Among the original trustees were William Barratt, proprietor of Barratt's Gardens at St John's, George William Harrison, the corn factor who was to become Wakefield's first mayor in 1848, James Fawcett, a corn-miller, T M Carter, the brewer, and the rising ironfounder, Edward Green. In March 1845 funds were sufficient to buy a plot of land in Thornhill Street. Plans were prepared by Barnsley architect John Whitworth, who was himself a Methodist and who was reported to have given his services free. Harrison personally supervised its building. The school had an infant section under John Stephens and an upper school in the care of the headteacher, a Mr Godley of Cheltenham.

In 1844, perhaps buoyed by the opening of their new chapel, the Independents of Zion Chapel founded a day school under the umbrella of the British and Foreign School Society (Figure 75). Little has been found by way of record of its existence. It appears in the directories of 1857 and 1861 but is not recorded in that of 1867 or any later ones. When Zion opened a massive new Sunday School

NEW
DAY SCHOOL.

THE INHABITANTS OF WAKEFIELD ARE INFORMED THAT A

Day School for Children

OF BOTH SEXES,

AND CONDUCTED UPON THE PRINCIPLES OF THE

BRITISH AND FOREIGN SCHOOL SOCIETY,

Will be commenced in the

SPACIOUS SCHOOL ROOMS OF

ZION CHAPEL,

ON MONDAY NEXT, APRIL 15th, 1844.

An efficient MASTER and MISTRESS, from the MODEL SCHOOLS in London, have been engaged, and the TERMS being only

TWO-PENCE PER WEEK,

A substantial Education is thus placed within the reach of all Classes, of which it is hoped they will not be slow to avail themselves.

The SCHOOL will commence at NINE O'CLOCK in the MORNING, and close at TWELVE ; Re-open at HALF-PAST ONE O'CLOCK in the AFTER-NOON, and close at HALF-PAST FOUR.

Weekly Payments to be made every Monday Morning, and in advance.

J. ROBINSON, PRINTER, KIRKGATE, WAKEFIELD.

Figure 75: An advertisement for Zion Day School. *The John Goodchild Collection*

building in November 1868, it was said that there were no plans to use it as a day school. Calculating the number of school places available in 1871, members of Wakefield School Board referred to the new and largely unused schoolrooms at Zion. It seems that the day-school failed in competition with the purpose-built Holy Trinity schools nearby and because it was not subsidised, as Trinity's were, by any government grant.

Daniel Gaskell hoped to provide a non-sectarian day school for the children of artisans and tradesmen of limited means. In 1850 he bought the Orangery, the premises in Back Lane, which had closed as a commercial garden (Figure 76). Gaskell had already established such a school in Horbury in 1842 to ensure that the children of Horbury's poor were provided with elementary education free of charge and whatever their family's religious beliefs. The Orangery was extended to the east to provide a saloon and it opened as a day school in September 1850 with James See as its master. The premises were given to the trustees of Westgate Chapel and the western part of the garden became a burial ground. The chapel anniversary on 18 November 1850 was marked by the children from Gaskell's Horbury School joining those from the new Artisans' School for a feast. However, Gaskell's Wakefield venture was not a success. The Orangery was taken over by 1857 by James Dear, who had been the master at Zion School, and run as a private school. Later Dear returned to Zion, but at the time the 1867 directory was compiled he was running a school in Northgate.

In 1861 Mary Milner had an infants school at the Orangery, which the young

Figure 76: The Orangery in Back Lane. *The author*

George Gissing (1857-1903) attended, and Joseph Harrison ran a private school there which was, as it happens, also attended by the future novelist.

Wakefield Corporation gained responsibility for a school for the first time in 1870 when the newly rebuilt township school at Thornes came into its care after an exchange of property with Joseph Barker. Its mistress was allowed to live in the adjoining house for a nominal rent of a shilling a year and could charge up to 2d a week for each pupil, their number being restricted to a maximum of sixty. Sarah Ann Steele, appointed in 1870, was expressly forbidden to allow any clergyman or minister of religion of any denomination to give religious instruction.

A Roman Catholic elementary school

The first known references to a school at St Austin's Roman Catholic Church are in 1838 when children from the Catholic School are included in a report of a procession that June to mark the coronation of Queen Victoria. The report refers only to 'Sunday School children' although it is clear from the inclusion of the children from the Charity School and the National School that the list actually includes day schools. Statistics provided for a visit of the bishop later that year make it clearer that St Austin's school operated on weekdays. They refer to twenty boys and twenty-five girls being educated at the charity school in a room underneath the chapel and to this being supported by voluntary subscription. More of the school is known from a letter written by Father Francis Jaritt in 1848 to the Reverend Dr John Briggs (1788-1861) in which he says, 'I have an average attendance of about sixty. The accommodation is good – a large boarded room under the chapel. I have a S. master no S. mistress. He is a lay person and a married man. The annual expenses consist of the salary of the S. master, the purchase of books, pens etc. The children pay 1d per week each to the S.master. Besides that I allow him 6s per week, his lodgings, and coals. To meet the expense I have recourse to voluntary subscriptions. This last year did not clear all. I was obliged to close my school for some weeks. It is now open again.' Where the married schoolmaster lived is not known. However, the 1851 census shows James Newnham, the thirty-six-year-old schoolmaster at that time, living at the Presbytery.

By 1858, when ninety pupils were being accommodated in the single room, the need for a purpose-built school was recognised. In May a most ambitious four-day bazaar was held to raise funds for 'St Austin's Poor School'. Plans were drawn up by Davies and Tew of Chesterfield. On 25 April 1859 the foundation stone of the new school was laid by Charles Langdale (1787-1868), the chair of the Catholic Poor Schools Committee. Langdale was one of the first Catholics to enter Parliament and was MP for Beverley from 1833-1836 and for Knaresborough from 1837-1841. The buildings were opened by the Dr Briggs who had been appointed Bishop of Beverley in 1850, on 18 October 1859. The complex included both an infant classroom and a classroom for older boys and girls, each measuring sixty foot by twenty foot, and a convent, dedicated to St

Figure 77: St Austin's schools and convent. *St Austin's Church archives*

Joseph, which had a dining-room, parlour and kitchen and three bedrooms. It stood at the town centre end of Jacob's Well Lane (Figure 77).

Infant education and Samuel Wilderspin

Neither the Lancasterian nor the National School originally catered for children under the age of five. An infant school was founded in Wakefield in 1829 in the wake of the formation of the Infant School Society in London in 1824. One of the major pioneers of infant education, Samuel Wilderspin (1791-1866), was appointed as the Society's agent, to tour the country to open schools for children between the ages, normally, of two and six, which were to be run along his principles. The Wakefield school was in Quebec Street with Margaret Scarth as its first mistress. Whilst little record of it has remained, it is thought that it continued until 1848. A surviving copy of its cash account for 1842 in the John Goodchild Collection, shows that it was supported by Nonconformists and Anglicans alike (Figure 78).

Infant education gained some spur when, through the patronage of Daniel Gaskell, Wilderspin retired to Wakefield in 1848. He had already visited Wakefield in 1843 to lecture on infant education in the Music Saloon. His principles for teaching very young children emphasised the need for frequent changes of activity, physical exercise in the form of drill, the use of all the senses via, in

CASH ACCOUNT OF THE INFANTS' SCHOOL,
WAKEFIELD.

SUBSCRIPTIONS AND DONATIONS RECEIVED IN 1842.

	£.	s.	d.		£.	s.	d.
Mrs. J. P. Heywood,	1	0	0	Mr. G. W. Harrison,	0	10	0
Mrs. J. P. Heywood, Donation	5	0	0	Mr. Joseph Horner	0	5	0
Oliver Heywood, Esq.	1	0	0	Mr. James Holdsworth,	0	5	0
Miss Heywood,	1	0	0	Mr. Michael Sanderson,	0	5	0
William Leatham, Esq.	1	0	0	Mr. Michael Sanderson, Donation	0	2	6
Mrs. Leatham,	1	0	0	Mr. Benjamin Dixon,	0	5	0
W. H. Leatham, Esq.	1	0	0	Mr. John Scholey,	0	5	0
Mrs. W. H. Leatham,	1	0	0	Mr. John Scholey, Donation	0	5	0
Mr. John Spence,	1	0	0	Mr. George Willis,	0	5	0
Messrs. George Benington and Co.	1	0	0	Mrs. Bennett,	0	5	0
Mrs. Joseph Holdsworth,	0	10	0	Mrs. Bennett, Donation	0	2	6
Mrs. Joseph Holdsworth, Donation	0	10	0	Mr. J. Horsfall,	0	5	0
Mrs. Samuel Holdsworth, (New Wells,)	0	10	0	Mr. Robert Mackie,	0	5	0
Mr. Ebenezer Walker,	0	10	0	Mrs. S. Saville,	0	3	0
Mr. Twisleton Haxby,	0	10	0	Mr. John Child,	0	2	6
Mr. W. I. Hanson,	0	10	0	Mr. John Perkin,	0	2	6
Mr. Joshua Walker,	0	10	0				
Miss New,	0	10	0		£21	13	0

TREASURER'S ACCOUNT.

DR.	£.	s.	d.	CR.	£.	s.	d.
Balance on Hand last Year,	2	10	4	Master's and Assistant's Salary,	27	3	4
Subscriptions and Donations,	21	13	0	Rent,	11	10	0
Children's Pence and Rent of Room,	17	1	5	Sundry Tradesmen's Bills and Coals,	5	13	11
Balance due to Treasurer,	2	13	6				
	£44	7	3		£44	7	3

The inconvenience under which the School laboured at the issuing of the last Report, by the decease of the late Master, has had an injurious effect upon its operations during the past Year; but the Committee have now engaged a Teacher, who, they think, will be efficient in bringing the School to its former state of prosperity, and they have pleasure in stating that it is already increasing in Number and much improved.

The Committee would be glad if the School was more visited by its supporters and friends, as their attendance would be beneficial to it, although for a time it might not be so entirely satisfactory to themselves; they feel confident that this Institution is worthy of the best patronage and support of a benevolent public.

The Public Examination of the Children will take place in the School Room, Quebec Street, on Thursday, the 22nd of June, at Two o'Clock, and the attendance of the Subscribers and Friends is respectfully invited.

VISITORS.

MRS. J. P. HEYWOOD.
MRS. G. CRAVEN.
MRS. J. SPENCE.
MISS NEW.

MRS. G. W. HARRISON.
MRS. S. HOLDSWORTH.
MRS. J. CLARKSON.
MRS. W. I. HANSON.

COMMITTEE.

MR. G. W. HARRISON, *Treasurer.*

W. H. LEATHAM, Esq.
REV. J. D. LORRAINE.
MR. E. WALKER, SURGEON.
MR. G. CRAVEN.

MR. JOHN HOLDSWORTH.
MR. J. HALSTEAD.
MR. G. BENINGTON.
MR. A. MACKIE.

MR. J. SPENCE.
MR. T. HAXBY.
MR. S. FEARNSIDES.
MR. T. CLAYTON.

COMMITTEE ROOM, 20th JUNE, 1843.

Thomas Nichols & Sons, Printers, Northgate, Wakefield.

Figure 78: The accounts for 1842 for Wakefield Infants' School. *The John Goodchild Collection*

particular visual aids (wherever possible real objects rather than just paintings), and immediate relevance to the child. For example, when teaching about the dreams of Joseph in the Hebrew scriptures, he invited children to talk about their own dreams. Education, he believed, should be non-denominational and he was strongly opposed to teaching any creed or catechism. His ideal teacher (a male) required 'a tenor voice, a good deal of vivacity, and a pleasing countenance'). A playground was an essential component of Wilderspin's infant school and here, he believed, moral lessons would be implicit. (Schools were held to be, and perhaps still are, a means of countering delinquency.) Learning methods varied from chanting rhymes as a way of learning arithmetic to the observation and discussion of objects of natural history. Wilderspin continued to influence infant education in Wakefield. He was instrumental in founding an infant school in connection with Holy Trinity Church. He 'examined' infants in public, exhibiting his own methods, in the Music Saloon in 1850 (Holy Trinity) and 1857 (the Lancasterian School) and probably on other occasions. He died on 10 March 1866 and was buried in Thornes churchyard.

The Ragged Schools other schools for the poor or delinquent
From time to time there were special efforts to cater for the poorest of Wakefield children. A Ragged School was founded in 1849 in Pincheon Street by the Reverend James Taylor, who had been appointed Headmaster of the Grammar School in 1847. Because of a shortage of funds it catered solely for boys and may have held its classes in the evenings rather than during the day, an arrangement that would have allowed Taylor to take part in the teaching. The winter of 1850-51 saw an 'average' (sic) attendance of fifty to sixty boys. It closed, through a lack of money, after eight years. Another Wakefield Ragged School was founded, initially as a Sunday School, in 1866 by the Wakefield tea-dealer and grocer, George Cooke, in a rented room in Crown Court. Complaints from those with premises nearby about the dirty state of the pupils led to Cooke's finding a new room in the area of the Borough Market at a rent of £13 a year. The school catered for some sixty to eighty of Wakefield's poorest children. It developed as a day school but also held evening classes, the latter drawing children who worked in the factories and mills by day. In addition it provided religious services as the Chapel of the Destitute and ran a Band of Hope to promote temperance. Feckless mothers were taught 'domestic habits' and had the 'privilege' of being read to whilst learning to mend their family's garments. The school operated a Penny Bank. Volunteers from both Anglicans and Nonconformists assisted as teachers but, for a period, there was a salaried master as well. The school was funded by subscriptions from middle-class philanthropists or by the profits from charity bazaars or by its own capacity to earn. It provided its pupils with a free dinner, a little teaching in the 'Three R's' and, via its industrial section, experience in such profitable tasks as chopping firewood. making sacks, blacking boots or sewing chemises or pillowcases. Its children were excluded from attendance at any of the

denominational schools since their families were either 'too poor or too dissolute'. At an early meeting of the Wakefield School Board in 1871 it was said that the majority of children attended in the evening rather than during the day. There is little surviving record of what happened to the pupils after they had left although a report in 1873 shows that some, at least, went into service. How long it survived is not so far known.

There is scant evidence of the Industrial Schools which came and went in Wakefield. Industrial Schools (not to be confused with the penal institutions that bore the same name) first mooted in the seventeenth century, were intended to be self-supporting. In addition to being taught the three Rs, the children were occupied in productive work such as sewing, knitting, and laundry, which brought in an income for the school. Some schools, it appears, trained girls for domestic service.

A Female School of Industry was established at Eastmoor in 1811 by members of Salem Independent Chapel and was still in existence twenty years later. There was a Female School of Industry in Garden Street by 1814. A bazaar in the 'New School Room' at Sandal was advertised as for the benefit of the Sunday School and to found a School of Industry and an Infant School.

White's 1837 directory shows that there was a day school at the House of Correction, for the young offenders detained there. In 1851 it catered for 185 boys and fifteen girls. By 1853 it had a schoolmistress (Mary Ann Ainley) and four masters (C Winter, J Flockton, J Altree, and J Burden).

Private Schools

Private schools proliferated through much of the century reaching their zenith between 1840 and 1870 although their number diminished thereafter. Most were very small and were run in the owners' own homes. They were run by single individuals, mothers with their daughters, women with their sisters. No qualifications were necessary and the schools must have failed or survived according to their calibre and their fees. There were numerous ones in Wakefield some leaving little trace beyond names in the trade directories and sporadic advertisements in local papers. Henry Clarkson, the author of *Memories of Merry Wakefield*, who was born in 1801, writes of attending a 'dame school' on Brook's bank (where Back Lane joins Westgate) and of moving from there to a school run by the Independent minister, the Reverend Benjamin Rayson, in a building at the end of Salem Chapel Yard, George Street. Rayson, whose school was in existence by 1807, took girls as well as boys and, when Clarkson first went to him, was assisted by Cornelius Clarke. In 1807 Rayson determined to reduce the number of his pupils and open the school as a boarding establishment. One of his assistants, William Johnson, then opened a day school in premises in the *Cock and Swan Yard* in Westgate. Among Rayson's pupils was Pudsey-born Enoch Harrison (1796-1877) who went on to become an assistant to Rayson and then to take over the school himself by 1820. Harrison moved the school to the rooms under the

Baptist Chapel in George Street and subsequently built his own academy in Smyth Street where his son, E H Harrison, assisted him. His students included Titus Salt, the great industrialist who founded his mill and the workers' village at Saltaire, near Bradford, artist Thomas Hartley Cromek, the Wakefield industrialist Joseph Rhodes and John Sharp, son of the vicar of Wakefield. Harrison's son died in 1868 and the Academy was taken over by W A Porritt who advertised it as Smyth Street Academy and School of Science He had a second master and a drill master and offered a 'classical, commercial, mathematical and technical' education. By 1875 the school included the Ladies' Collegiate Academy.

George Laurence, one of the masters from the Proprietory School, established a school in Chestnut Grove in 1854, moving to Galway House, Westgate the same year and to Alverthorpe Hall in 1855 where he had six assistant masters, five dormitories and thirty beds. However by 1858 he was bankrupt. Heath Hall housed a boarding school for young ladies in the 1820s run by a Miss Simpson.

Clergy in particular seem to have needed to augment their income by taking pupils. The minister at Westgate Chapel, Thomas Johnstone, advertised for pupils in 1811. A successor, the Reverend Edward Higginson, advertised in 1847 that he would teach pupils in his home or theirs at four shillings an hour preparing them for the professions or commercial life. Richard Cope, minister at Salem until 1829 and subsequently minister to a congregation in Quebec Street, had a school in Southgate.

The School Board
Arguably, the most significant event in the history of Education nationally was the passing of the Education Act of 1870, usually referred to as the 'Foster Act' because it was piloted through Parliament by the Bradford MP, Edward Foster. It led a few years later, once sufficient school places were available, to compulsory Education. Although Government grants had been available for voluntary schools for many years, it marked the first real move to state secular Education. Foster's Act provided for the setting up of democratically elected School Boards in any local government area where the voluntary schools could not cater for all the child population. The Boards were authorised to make a precept on the rates and to build elementary schools.

In fact by 1870, Wakefield was comparatively well served. Nonetheless, immediately after the passing of the Act, the Mayor of Wakefield, Alderman Samuel Whitham, seized the initiative, calling a special meeting of the Town Council and laying a motion before it to petition the Privy Council for a School Board for Wakefield. The motion was passed by just one vote. Controversy started to rage within the Council and beyond. There were public meetings, persuasive placards, and hectoring handbills for and against the instigation of a Board. Members of the Established Church, determined to have the major influence on the Board, held meetings to select five candidates for the nine places. One of

Wakefield's leading figures at the time, the industrialist Edward Green, was one of the voices raised against the idea. Insisting that Wakefield had enough schools already, he said the Board would prove a costly business and that it would be better to wait to see how things developed elsewhere before taking so bold a step in Wakefield. Knowing that School Boards had the power to make Education compulsory, other opponents argued that no child should be made to attend school if parents objected. They feared, too, with some foresight, that the step would lead ultimately to free education for all at the ratepayers' expense. The keenest supporter of the School Board was the Reverend John Sheppard Eastmead, then minister of Salem Congregational Chapel. He regarded the spread of education as a means of countering 'pauperism, ignorance and crime' and thought a rate of threepence in the pound would be sufficient to pay for all that was needed. Both Green, the opponent, and Eastmead, the supporter, were elected to the nine-strong School Board in January 1871. Before the election, when Wakefield ratepayers voted for their School Board, parties were formed. There was rivalry for places amongst the clergy whilst denominational interests were blurred by political ones. The Church of England fielded four official candidates, Edward Green amongst them. No clergy figured in this official list so the Vicar of Thornes, the Reverend Henry Jones, stood unofficially. He was elected largely because of the massive support in his own Calder Ward. Besides Green, Jones and Eastmead, who had stood as one of three undenominational candidates (Father Robert Cooper, St Austin's immensely popular parish priest standing in the Catholic interest and Alderman W H Lee) the other official Anglican candidates were elected, Councillor W H B Tomlinson, Councillor John Connor, and Mr Robert Barratt. Filling the final place on the Board was the Mayor, Alderman Whitham, who had started the ball rolling and was elected to the Board as the third undenominational candidate.

At the first meeting, on 16 February 1871, Edward Green was somewhat ironically elected chairman. The Board met regularly on the first Tuesday of each month in the Council Chamber of the old Town Hall in Crown Court. Its first step was to select a design for its seal. It chose a motif of Wisdom teaching the young designed by Wakefield artist Louisa Fennell. A survey of existing provision in the town indicated that about 800 children under the age of five, and 3,200 between the ages of five and thirteen were receiving some kind of elementary education in day schools paying fees of between twopence and fourpence a week. For the majority the curriculum focused on reading, writing, arithmetic, dictation and religious education. Most girls were also taught needlework. Other subjects included geography, drawing, natural history, history, singing, and music. It was estimated on the basis of the 1871 census that Wakefield, with a population then of 28,071, had 350 children aged between five and thirteen who were receiving no education at all. As early as July 1871 the Board decreed that all children in Wakefield between the ages of five and thirteen must attend a school. In this Wakefield was in the forefront of the national situation. Joseph Brooke was appointed as school warden to make sure that they did so. In cases where parents could not afford the weekly fee, the Board would pay for them on the warden's advice. Parents who ignored the ruling would be prosecuted.

Education became compulsory nationally only under the 1880 Act when the leaving age was still only ten.

The Board's ruling making education compulsory had a positive effect on the schools provided by the religious bodies. In the 1870s schools could 'earn' twelve shilling a year for each pupil passing the Inspector's tests. As more children attended regularly, the schools fared better financially. Even at the end of the century, however, average attendance was less than ideal, rising from 60% in 1871 to 82% in 1897. Compulsory attendance also meant that schools could become overcrowded. St Austin's new school was unable to cope with the increase and the boys returned in July 1872 to the old schoolrooms under St Austin's Church. An extension was built on the Teall Street site and was consecrated by the Roman Catholic bishop in June 1873.

Not surprisingly in view of the composition of the Board, it was over eighteen months later before it set to work seriously to meet the shortfall in school places. Plans were drawn up by Wakefield architect William Watson for a new school in Westgate in November 1872 and, after the scheme gained approval from the Government's Board of Education, George Fawcett was commissioned to build it in March 1873. The foundation stone was laid on 8 September 1873 by the Board's chairman, Edward Green.

In its first years the School Board might be described as 'laid back' but James Eastmead, one of the most regular attenders at its meetings, prodded it on so that it became a more efficient and professional body. It went on to organise evening continuation classes, to negotiate the training of pupil teachers, and even to institute checks on pupils' eyesight. The Board's second school, and the only one which remains in use in the twenty-first century, was built on Eastmoor Road (Figure 79). This followed the opening of Park Hill Colliery and the building of 176 houses in the Selby Street area by colliery owner George Bradley. Although an additional school was being built in Clarendon Street for St John's, and St Austin's had been enlarged, it was clear in 1876 that another school would be needed. Under pressure from Eastmead, the Board agreed to buy a site belonging to timber merchants Roberts and Smith facing the Pauper Lunatic Asylum, despite concern that the inmates would lure schoolchildren into running errands for them. William Watson was again commissioned as the architect. A Normanton builder, James Webster, undertook the work. In April 1877 there was a procession from the Town Hall to the site of the new school where Mrs Edward Green laid the foundation stone while pupils from Westgate Board School sang All people that on earth do dwell. The school opened on 11 March 1878. Nearly twenty years later, the Board undertook what was to be its finest achievement, the building of Ings Road School. Since the building of the Westgate and Eastmoor schools, interest in the design of elementary school buildings had become much

Figure 79: Eastmoor School. *The author*

stronger. Space, light and air were regarded as critical factors and the nine classrooms at Ings Road were arranged so that light could fall at each desk over the pupil's left shoulder. The school catered fully for pupils up to Standard Seven.

The first member the School Board to represent the Labour interest was James Walsh, a checkweighman at Park Hill Colliery, who was a Roman Catholic and joined the Board in 1895. A jeweller, Fred Land, who, as it happens was a Conservative, was elected to the Board at the same time to represent the Roman Catholics.

In 1895 it was reported that 347 children from outlying townships attended schools in Wakefield. Towards the end of 1900, when the boundary of Wakefield was extended, the Board became responsible for Willow Lane School, Alverthorpe taking it over from the defunct Alverthorpe School Board.

Adult education

An early venture to provide adult education for working men was promoted by the ubiquitous Martin Naylor. In 1824 Naylor led moves to found a Mechanics Institution. This was short lived. A Literary and Scientific Society was formed in the 1830s. In 1836 the Literary and Philosophical Society, founded in 1827, had talks on subjects ranging from Prison Discipline to Spontaneous Combustion, the latter regarded as 'involved in much obscurity' and being illustrated by 'cases of doubtful character'!). In March 1838, a Geological and Polytechnic Society was formed at a meeting in the Music Saloon with the intention of bringing together coal owners to understand the geology of the area. In 1838 the Reverend J Cameron, minister at Westgate Chapel, formed a Working Men's Educational Society which was in part political and supported Chartism.

A second, more firmly based, Wakefield Mechanics Instititution was formed in 1841 with the object of supplying 'to the working classes of Wakefield the means of instruction in Science, Literature and the Arts'. It was to be both apolitical and secular. Its rules, adopted in 1843, state that 'no political or religious subject shall be introduced at any of the Society's meetings'. However it quickly came under the domination of Wakefield's Liberal faction. Membership was open to both men and women with a reduced subscription for those under eighteen. The Institution met initially in the Assembly Rooms in Crown Court but within a year of its inception, it leased the Music Saloon in the Public Rooms in Wood Street. Classes were held in the 1840s in Reading, Writing and Arithmetic, Book-keeping, Mechanics, Architectural Drawing, Practical Philosophy (for the acquisition of scientific knowledge), Geography, German, Phonography and Phonographic Reporting. This last was the system of shorthand that Isaac Pitman had introduced in 1837. The 1847-8 Report shows that Reading, Writing and Arithmetic was by far the most popular class with an average attendance of thirty-three men and twenty-three women.

Since the committee of the Mechanics Institution was made up of Nonconformists, it is scarcely surprising that in 1845 a rival Institution was established in the town by the leaders of the Church of England. At the inaugural meeting, held in the Court House in Wood Street on 24 October, the Reverend Dr Scoresby, vicar of Bradford, referred to the 'ignorance, not least of the distinctive principles of the Church of England, which led to people being seduced by religious dissent and by Roman Catholicism'. Dr Scoresby proposed that the objects of the new Institution should be

> the maintenance and advancement of the principles of the Church of England, the promotion of General Knowledge in subordination to religion, the cultivation of Church Music, and the encouragement of kindly intercourse between all classes of churchmen.

The Church already feared at this time that the teaching of Geology, unless it were 'in subordination to religion' would conflict with the understanding of the Book of Genesis and might even lead to atheism.

Rooms were taken in the building lying between King Street and Crown Court which was later to be leased to Wakefield Corporation as its Town Hall. The library from the parish church was transferred there.

Figure 80: The Church Institute. *Yorkshire Archaeological Society*

Figure 81: Wakefield
Technical and Art College.
The author's collection

The Mechanics Institution and the Church Institution came into direct rivalry when the Public Rooms in Wood Street came on the market in 1855. Both bodies determined to buy it. The Mechanics Institution had rented rooms there from 1842. Its committee outbid the Anglicans and it acquired the building for £3,000 although for some years two of the ground-floor rooms remained in use by the public news room and a subscription library and the Music Saloon remained available for a wide variety of functions.

Later the same year the committee of the Church Institution acquired a site in Marygate and commissioned plans for a new building from William Dykes, architect son of William Hey Dykes, who was practising in York. Two years later the adjacent site was also purchased. There were no funds available to make further progress, however. Then, in 1858, the Crown Court premises were burnt out. Following William Dykes's death, Alfred Burdekin Higham drew up new plans for an Institute. Eventually, on 27 May 1861, the foundation stone of the Church Institute was laid by the Bishop of Ripon. The Institute was opened on 22 June 1862 (Figure 80). It had a newsroom, a library, a lecture hall seating 500, class rooms and a picture gallery. It provided classes in the reading, writing, and arithmetic, and a form of shorthand was also taught. There were lectures on whatever the speakers chose to offer.

The Church Institute was financed by donations, subscriptions and an annual bazaar held in the Corn Exchange. It survived into the twentieth century but finally closed in 1930 when the building was sold.

Evening classes were provided for a period from October 1866 at the Lancasterian School but the following year they were merged with those at the Mechanics Institute. The Parish Church also provided evening classes at this time.

The Wakefield College of the twenty-first century owes its origins to the setting up of the School of Art and Craft in 1868. This was founded, in part, from the profits of the Wakefield Industrial and Fine Art Exhibition of 1865. Where the Mechanics Institution was dominated by Nonconformists and the Church Institution was explicitly Anglican, the School of Art and Craft was founded 'on the basis of equality for all parties and denominations'. In 1888 there was an appeal for funds for a technical school. The foundation stone was laid in March 1890 by the Sir Edward Green and the building was opened by the Duke of Clarence on 30 April 1891. Wakefield Corporation took over the Technical and Art School in 1900 (Figure 81).

Boys from the Green Coat School who were apprenticed to Wakefield tradespeople under the Bromley endowment were, from 1846, expected to attend an Apprentice School on Sundays and on Monday (later Wednesday) evenings. Under the bequest, the young men were provided with clothing and, if they finished their term, they were given a premium. The register of apprentices who attended the school between 1846 and 1863, includes brief comments, pasted into it, and written presumably by the teacher. At least one young man wasted his premium: James Nichols, who had been bound to a joiner, William Lund, obtained his money and 'repaired to a brothel where at last he was found by the chief constable'. Thomas Tate, on the other hand, 'finished his time and went to Australia' where he became 'clerk of a church and master of a choir' near Melbourne. Going abroad seems to have had its attractions. The register shows one young man 'badly advised by his relatives' who quit his apprenticehip with Joseph Thornton, a tailor, to seek his fortune in America. James Wraith was persuaded by his Master, the wheelwright Edward Mitchell, to accompany him to America. The teacher notes that he was doing well there and had sent for his mother to join him. Robert Hey, who was apprenticed to Amon Ellis, a machine maker, enlisted rather than continue with his apprenticeship and saw service in India. 'His father kept a beer house in New Street much frequented by soldiers', reports the teacher.

Sources

Frank Smith, *A History of English Elementary Education, 1760-1902*, 1931.

Sandra Hargreaves, 'The Black Bull or Great Bull Inn of Wakefield,' *Wakefield Historical Society Journal*, Volume 13, 2004.

R B Chapman, *A History of Queen Elizabeth Grammar School*, Wakefield, 1992.

Matthew Peacock, *History of Wakefield Grammar School*, 1928.

John Wilkinson, *For Grammar and other Good Learning*, 1991.

S J Curtis and M E A Boultwood, *An Introductory History of English Education since 1800*, 1960.

Harold Speak and Jean Forrester, *Education in Wakefield 1275-1970, an Outline History.* 1970.

Diane Exley, *Chalking up Progress: 160 years of state-assisted education in Wakefield*, 1993.

Edward Baines, *The Social, Educational and Religious State of the Manufacturing Districts*, 1843.

Phillip McCann, and Francis Young, *Samuel Wilderspin and the Infant School Movement*, 1982.

Papers relating to St Andrew's schools at the West Yorkshire Archive Service, Wakefield.

Dennis McKniff: *A History of St Austin's Church, Wakefield, 1828-1931*, 1991.

George Cooke, Report of the Ragged School for the year ending 13 October 1867.

Wakefield Apprentice School register, 1844-1878, West Yorkshire Archive Service.

Clifford Brooke, 'Wakefield Mechanics' Institution', *Wakefield Historical Society*, Volume 6, 1979

6 $\mathscr{L}$EISURE AND ENTERTAINMENT

In 1801 there were few places of entertainment in Wakefield and, as far as can be discerned,comparatively few, other than private, social gatherings. There were occasional balls and concerts in the Assembly Rooms attached to the *White Hart Hotel*, opposite the parish church, in Westgate. Here there was a hall measuring sixty-two foot by twenty-two foot and a card room. There were similar functions at the new Assembly Rooms which had been built in the George and Crown Yard in 1798. This latter was probably the venue known sometimes as the Music Hall. Here, on 17 December 1801, there were day-long festivities to mark the expected Peace of Amiens, with performances from oratorios starting at 11am to a concert and ball beginning at 7pm. Throughout the century there were modest numbers of balls and concerts during the winter seasons, sometimes on a subscription basis. Sometimes these were provided by entrepreneurs such as Percival Phillips (1783-1860) who ran a business in Westgate as a music seller and put on concerts, for example,at the White Hart Assembly Rooms in the 1820s. Concerts were, in particular in the second half of the century, sometimes regarded as an important means of 'improving' the working classes. One W L Robinson personally sponsored seasons of concerts for the Mechanics Institute in 1851-2. These were designed to 'provide a good musical entertainment at a much lower rate than had previously been afforded and to develop the musical taste of the town and its neighbourhood'. There were the bi-annual fairs which brought varied entertainments. And there was the theatre.

The nineteenth century saw new public buildings, sports grounds and swimming baths, a proliferation of voluntary groups with a common interest in sport or some form of trade or culture, social provision at churches and chapels, and an increase in commercial entertainment. Railways provided the adventure of comparatively cheap and easy excursions. The 1890s brought Wakefield a new theatre which is thriving in the twenty-first century. The leading twentieth-century entertainment, moving pictures, came to Wakefield before the century's end.

Theatres and Music Halls

The original theatre, on the same site in Westgate where the 1894 Theatre Royal and Opera House still stands, had been opened in 1776 (Figure 82). Built on his own land by James Banks, a woolstapler, who lived at the nearby York House, the theatre was leased until his death in 1803 to Tate Wilkinson, the actor-manager who operated the York Circuit. Wilkinson's company spent the year moving

Figure 82: The original theatre. *Yorkshire Archaeological Society*

through their circuit, travelling by waggon, on horseback or on foot, playing at their 'head' theatre in York, and visiting Hull, Leeds, Doncaster, Pontefract and Wakefield where it stayed normally for only a fortnight, in September. Wilkinson also made occasional forays elsewhere – to Halifax in particular. Writing in his memoirs, *The Wandering Patentee*, Wilkinson described his visits to Wakefield as always 'attended with welcome, benevolence and success'. He remarked that, 'In all my circuit, I have not a more spirited or liberal audience, and the attendants at the gallery more numerous and full of alacrity to make their appearance than at Wakefield.' The theatre, which had a rectangular auditorium, held people from all walks of society, with the gallery – cheaper than elsewhere – patronised by the lower classes. The boxes, along three sides, were taken by the middle classes and gentry, and the pit (simply rows of benches in the centre of the hall) held artisans and the lower middle class.

In its earliest years, performances at the theatre took place on the evening of race days. The races were held on the Wakefield Outwood, on a course lying between Lawns Lane, Lofthouse Beck and the Wakefield-Bradford turnpike road. Although racing came to an end in 1794, following the Wakefield Inclosure Act, Wilkinson maintained the practice of playing at Wakefield in the corresponding September period.

Following Wilkinson's death, his son, John, ran the circuit until 1814, still bringing his company for the short September season. The circuit then had a series of short-lived lessee-managers, all again normally bringing their companies to Wakefield just for two or three weeks in September and all providing much the same fare – comedy, tragedy, farce and pantomime or Harlequinade as it was sometimes called. The programme changed each evening. There were two principal, contrasting, items and a shorter entertainment between them. For example one evening in 1819 saw Shakespeare's *King Lear* and the pantomime of *Cinderella*. On 17 May 1833 *Othello* was followed by a dance by Master Saunders, gymnastic contortions by Signor Koellanco, and *The Spectre Bridegroom* by Moncrieff.

Some indication of the standing of the theatre can be derived from the names of the men and women, or groups, who gave their patronage to individual performances and whose names head the playbills. In the 1780s and 1790s, Tate Wilkinson enjoyed many patrons amongst the gentry whose town houses lay in Westgate or whose handsome villas stood in their own grounds on the periphery of the town. Patrons were able to 'bespeak', or choose, the programme and were expected to lavish tickets upon their friends. In the nineteenth century there were fewer bespeaks and the standing of the theatre dropped, in part because of an element of puritanical opposition to playgoing. However, Godfrey Wentworth of Woolley Hall was a patron on one occasion in 1818. In 1823, after the theatre was fitted for gas lighting, the Wakefield Gas Company gave its patronage. Other patrons in the remaining days of the York Circuit included Arthur Heywood of Stanley Hall, Daniel Gaskell of Lupset Hall, John Pemberton Heywood of

THE LAST WEEK.

By Desire and under the Patronage of the
WORSHIPFUL THE MASTER,
OFFICERS, AND BRETHREN,
OF THE LODGE OF UNANIMITY OF
Free and Accepted Masons.

THEATRE, WAKEFIELD.

On MONDAY Evening, January 2nd, 1837,

Will be presented the admired Comedy of

SECRETS
WORTH KNOWING.

Written by T. Morton, Esq. Author of "Speed the Plough," &c.

Rostrum,......Mr. SMEDLEY.   April,......Mr. ROGERS.
Undermine,..Mr. NEVILLE.   Nicholas,..Mr. LOCKWOOD.   Greville,..Mr. LACEY.
Plethora,..Mr. REID.   Egerton,..Mr. MONTAGUE.   Valet,..Mr. CAMERON.
Coachman,....Mr. SHELDON.   Cook,....Master G. SMEDLEY.
Mrs. Greville,....Miss NEVILLE.   Rose Sidney,....Miss SMEDLEY.
Sally Downright,............Mrs. LOCKWOOD.

MR. LOCKWOOD WILL SING "JOLLY CHRISTMAS."
"THE SEVEN AGES OF WOMAN," BY MR. REID.

To conclude with a laughable FARCE, called

My Uncle John
AND HIS COUSINS.

Uncle John,......Mr. NEVILLE.   Nephew Hawk,......Mr. MONTAGUE.
Friend Thomas,......Mr. ROGERS.   Edward Easel,......Mr. MOSLEY.
William,......Mr. CAMERON.   Andrew,......Mr. REID.   John,......Mr. SHELDON.
Niece Hawk....Miss A. SMEDLEY.   Eliza,....Miss DESBOROUGH.
Mrs. Comfort,....Mrs. LOCKWOOD.

Nights of Performance, which will be the last, Monday, Wednesday, Thursday, and Friday.

Doors to be opened at Half-past Six, and the Performance to commence at Seven precisely.

BOXES, 3s.—PIT, 2s.—GALLERY, 1s.

Children under 12 Years of age admitted at the commencement, to
BOXES, 2s.—PIT, 1s.—GALLERY, 6d.

Second Price, Boxes, 2s.   Pit, 1s.   Gallery 6d.

Tickets may be had of the Printers, of Mr. Smedley, and at the Theatre, where Places for the Boxes may be taken.

ROWLAND HURST, PRINTER, WESTGATE, WAKEFIELD.

Figure 83: A playbill for 2 January 1837. *The author's collection*

Wentworth House, the members of the Gentlemen's book club, the officers of the Lower Agbrigg Troop of Yeomen Cavalry, and the Freemasons (Figure 83).

The break with the York Circuit came in 1835 when Joseph Smedley (1784-1863) leased, and in 1839 bought, the theatre. Smedley had begun company management on his own account about 1806 when he leased the theatre in Grimsby. He had toured for many years with his small band of twelve or so players, primarily in the small market towns of Nottinghamshire and Lincolnshire but had clearly decided that the growing industrial towns of the West Riding might be more profitable. Until 1845, when licensing was applied to theatre buildings, companies of players had to secure a licence from the magistrates for the company for each venue where they appeared. In 1833 Smedley held more licences than any other actor-manager in the country. In the mid 1830s he secured licences from the West Riding magistrates to play in Barnsley, Bradford, Huddersfield, Pontefract and Rotherham as well as Wakefield. His company played in Wakefield from late October until early January. In his first season he secured the patronage of the then Constable of Wakefield, John Barff.

Smedley retired from the theatre in 1841 (to run a business as a printer in Sleaford) but continued to own the theatre until his death in 1863. Despite the efforts of a series of short-lived lessees, the fortunes of the theatre languished. For many of the middle classes theatrical entertainment was no longer regarded as respectable (despite Queen Victoria's appreciation of it). Lower class theatre-goers seem to have included rowdy and trouble-making elements. In 1845, the lessees announced:

> *Notice is hereby given that persons entering the theatre in a state of intoxication, smoking, throwing orange peel, nut shells etc, shouting, or personally addressing the musicians or other individuals in the theatre, or in any way disturbing or annoying the audience, will be instantly removed by the constables who are in constant attendance to keep order.* Playbill, 2 December 1845

A decade later *The Wakefield Journal and Examiner* observed that 'A distinction is now drawn between the drama and the theatre, and this is shown by the popularity of dramatic readings while the theatres remain empty.'

The coming of railway travel brought a major change to provincial theatres, albeit only slowly at first, resulting in the demise of the circuit companies. Professional groups could travel the length of the country to bring a particular production, possibly one that originated in London, for just one or two nights. In Wakefield the first example of this was when the Metropolitan and Provincial Dramatic Company came in June 1855 for two nights with *Used Up* by Dion Boucicault and *Eugene Aram*, a play based on the life of the Knaresborough murderer taken from the novel by Edward George Bulwer-Lytton.

The first season of opera in Wakefield occurred in 1858 when the Metropolitan Grand Opera Company appeared at the theatre for six nights in July, drawing, unusually in that period, a 'fashionable' audience.

The theatre was occasionally taken by local, and probably short-lived, amateur groups. In April 1823 the Theatrical Amateurs of Wakefield gave a performance of *Pizarro*. In March 1825, the Gentlemen Amateurs of Wakefield put on *The Rivals* in aid of the widows and children of those who had died in the Gosforth Pit disaster at Middleton Colliery on 14 January. In 1826 the Shakespeare Society gave a number of performances in April and May including a benefit for the House of Recovery and the Wakefield Dispensary. On 15 May 1854 amateurs paid £15s to hire the theatre for a single night for a benefit for the wives and children of soldiers fighting in the Crimea. They performed plays with a military resonance: Shakespeare's tragedy of *Othello* and, as the after-piece, *The Noble Soldier*. A thin audience brought an income of only £4 7s 4d but the overall expenses were £5 6s 6d. At Christmas 1858 members of the Wakefield Dramatic Institution performed *The Lost Son* and *Alice, the Betrothed* on 24 December and *The Lady of Lyons* and *Two Faces under one Hood* on 27 December. The anonymous author of the last play was, so the theatre's first historian, William Senior noted, a Wakefield man, George Atkinson, who went on to be the Town Clerk of Liverpool. Wakefield Dramatic Society took the theatre for two nights, in July and December, in 1860. In 1863 a group from the Leeds Rifle Volunteers appeared on the Wakefield stage in February and in December. On the last occasion it was commented that, 'The less said about the performance the better', and 'a very respectable and pretty large audience was heartily sick of the whole affair.'

After Smedley's death in 1863, the theatre was sold to Nathan Webster, described in the deeds as a 'comedian' or actor, who renamed it the Alhambra and ran it as a music hall. The music halls of the 1850s and 60s had developed from the free-and-easies, or sing-songs, associated with the rapidly growing number of urban public houses. They had their origin in a working-class culture and the early performers were local amateurs. *The Victoria Inn*, in Kirkgate, advertised 'music, singing and dancing' in 1870. Whether the performers were professional or not is unknown. But professional artistes emerged and singing saloons paved the way for purpose-built popular concert rooms where patrons could sit and drink and enjoy the acts. Glimpses of the Alhambra can be found in encounters with the magistrates rather than from handbills or advertisements in the papers. When Webster applied for a theatre licence in 1865 the magistrates objected that he already had an ale licence and drink could not be sold in premises licensed for theatrical performances. At the hearing, the Chief Constable, James McDonnold, reported that the entertainment took the form of 'poses plastiques' or tableaux but that there was no nudity. In the same year a coal-miner, who was charged with drunkenness and riotous conduct, said that he had been playing dominoes at 'T'lambra singing hoyle'. Three years later, a woman artiste appeared before the magistrates charged with assaulting Webster when he allowed a rival performer on the stage.

Pantomimes as Christmas entertainment were a Victorian novelty, with spectacular scenery, large casts of child dancers and plots based on fairy tales. The first one to be performed in Wakefield (as far as is known) was put on at the theatre the Christmas season 1868-69 when William Charles Middleton, from Dewsbury, succeeded in obtaining a theatre licence.

In the first half of the century, vacant land between King Street and Wood Street provided a site for both visiting circuses and portable theatres, often at the time of the July or September fair. Mrs Wild's theatre was set up in Wood Street for several weeks in the winter of 1842-3. The Constable, George W Harrison, who was later to become Wakefield's first mayor, complained to the magistrates that great numbers of disorderly boys and girls congregated there each night. Thompson's Theatre came in 1846 and William Schuking Thorne brought his theatre in 1849 and immediately afterwards leased the permanent theatre for a short time. In 1851 the July fair brought the theatres of both J P Edwards and a Mr Johnstone. In the second half of the century, portable theatres and other shows were moved to the area of the Borough Market. Edwards operated what he now advertised as his New Borough Market Theatre in the 1850s. In June 1857, Edwin Blanchard, who had leased the Westgate Theatre at the time and clearly resented the competition, brought a charge against Sam Wild for operating a portable theatre in Wakefield without a licence. S A Pickuls applied to build a theatre behind the Borough Market in 1867.

The original theatre in Westgate was sold in September 1883 to Benjamin Sherwood (1847-1926), then licensee of the *Crown and Anchor* in Kirkgate where he ran a music hall named successively the People's Music Hall, and the Gaiety. Sherwood's intention was to revive the theatre as a venue for the middle class giving it again a respectable cultural image. He relied from the outset on bringing touring companies, included nationally-acclaimed opera companies. Indeed in January 1884 he secured the Carl Rosa Opera Company for a week although the stage proved far too small for the ensemble. At Christmas 1885 the D'Oyly Carte Opera Company provided a repertoire that included its latest comic opera, *The Mikado*. Sherwood was able to boast an impressive range of patrons including Lord St Oswald of Nostell Priory and the new industrial magnates, Edward Green, of the Fuel Economiser works and of Heath Old Hall, Percy Tew, banker, of Woolgreaves, C E Charlesworth, colliery owner, of Moor House, Stanley, Colonel Mackie, cornfactor, of Manor House, Heath, W T Marriott, worsted spinner of Sandal Grange, T K Sanderson, maltster and cornfactor of South Parade, and H M Carter, brewer, of Fairground Road (George Street).

But Sherwood's success was not to last long. The newly-created County Council took over the responsibility for licensing theatres from the magistrates in 1889 and Sherwood was compelled to make a number of alterations, to meet the County Surveyor's demands, before obtaining a renewal of his licence. Then, in 1890, came serious competition with the opening of 'Baron Antonio's' Grand Circus in Teall Street on 29 September. The Circus, unlike the portable theatres,

Figure 84: The rebuilt theatre of 1894. The extension on the left was added in 1905.
The author's collection

was a substantial wooden building, designed and constructed by T V Woodhouse of Nottingham. Measuring ninety foot by seventy foot, it was said to be capable of holding 2,000 people in galleries, a pit, cushioned stalls, and a promenade. There was, it was claimed, 'good accommodation for artistes and horses'. Entertainment at the Circus was provided in turn by Edward Croueste and by James Comerford who used the professional name of Zaro.

The D'Oyly Carte Opera Company, having evidently found the old theatre unsuitable, brought *The Yeomen of the Guard* to the Corn Exchange in September 1889 and *The Gondoliers* in November 1890. There was competition, too, from the Gaiety Music Hall, now run by Mrs A Lawrenson, and the *London Hotel* in Kirkgate, each of which had licences for professional music and dancing. In 1893 both the *Borough Market Hotel* in Westmorland Street and the *Khedive Hotel* in William Street obtained similar licenses.

In 1892 the County Council refused to renew Sherwood's stage-play licence. The Surveyor saw the theatre as a fire hazard: the staircases were of wood, there was a six-foot area either side of the stage which was filled with discarded properties and refuse and there was no safety curtain. Sherwood had the choice of making considerable alteration to the existing, and now outmoded, theatre or to build an entirely new one. He opted for the latter, engaging Britain's foremost theatre architect, Frank Matcham, for the task. The new Theatre Royal and Opera House opened on 15 October 1894 (Figure 84).

At the same time the Teall Street Circus was taken over by Will Hebden who ran it as a highly popular music hall, renaming it the People's Empire, and providing a competition that was a serious threat to Sherwood's business. Hebden was followed by Fred Harcourt who, in April 1897, brought the great novelty moving pictures to Wakefield for the first time. Before the end of the year Benjamin Sherwood had acquired the People's Empire to stifle the competition, and closed it down. It became an immense advertising hoarding.

Balls and bazaars
The second of the great public buildings in Wood Street was built in the 1820s and included, as its principal feature, a first-floor salon, where balls, concerts and other entertainments were held for well over a hundred years. Planned as Public Rooms and primarily as a philanthropic enterprise, it was built following a public meeting of 20 January 1820. The intention was to provide 'newsroom, library, dwelling house for a librarian, and other rooms'. The Reverend Samuel Sharp, vicar of Wakefield, was prominent among its promoters. Shares were offered at £25. A committee was set up and a deposit paid on a site in Wood Street still owned by the Reverend William Wood. Although the take-up of shares was slow at first (and there was a public notice in July 1820 berating the people of Wakefield for their failure to come up to the standard of Leeds) the full price of the site had been raised by late 1820. The building was designed by one of Yorkshire's leading architectural practices, Watson and Pritchett of York. The foundation stone was laid on 13 November 1820 followed by a dinner at the *Woodman Inn* on the opposite side of Wood Street. On the ground floor were a reading room, the anticipated news room, a ladies' room, and a card room. For some years, Wakefield Dispensary occupied a part of the basement.

The building work took many months. Before it was completed, in the darkness on 16 November 1821, twenty-nine-year-old William Webber, a clown in Cooke's Olympic Circus which was visiting Wood Street at the time, fell into the unprotected 'area' (the well giving light to the cellar) and broke his neck. The Coroner criticised the Street Commissioners for failing to ensure the safety of the site and fined the proprietors £20 unless the building was made safe within eighteen hours.

The name of Music Saloon was first applied to the concert hall in the Public Rooms when it opened in December 1823 (Figure 85). Much later the whole building came to be known by that name. The saloon was by no means filled for the opening concert but for the second one, on 19 January 1824, it was packed to overflowing. The attraction was Angelica Catalani (1780-1949), an operatic soprano 'of the greatest possible fame' by now past her best years but still evidently a great draw. Ticket prices were high, 8s in the body of the hall and 5s in the gallery. A second appearance, on 26 January, was hastily arranged.

Figure 85: The Public Rooms. *Yorkshire Archaeological Society*

The opening of the Music Saloon must have contributed to the plan to hold a great Musical Festival – the first (and last) of its kind in Wakefield – in 1824. Behind the scheme was the redoubtable vicar of Wakefield, Samuel Sharp. The enterprise was probably also prompted by the fact that there had been a festival in Sandal Church in September 1823 and a four-day festival in York in October 1823 which included concerts, and balls, as well as the opening of the theatre. The Wakefield Festival lasted three days, from Wednesday, 29 September to Friday, 1 October. There were performances of sacred music each morning in the parish church, concerts on the first evenings in the Music Saloon, and in the Court House, dedicated to 'ancient' music, on the second night. There was a ball on the final evening. Apart from bringing some culture to Wakefield, the aim was to raise funds for local charities. However the plans were over ambitious. National stars of the day were engaged to perform and the York architects, Atkinson and Sharp, were commissioned to introduce an additonal gallery, in the church chancel, with twenty-seven rows of benches to hold 550 people and accessed by two staircases. The church was festooned throughout with crimson cloth. The theatre was opened specially during the same week rather to provide additional entertainment than to compete with the Festival itself. Whilst the events were well attended, there were insufficient numbers for its charitable purpose. *The Leeds Mercury* remarked at its conclusion that the proceeds were unlikely to pay the expenses. There was a further musical event in the parish church in June 1829 to raise funds for the repair of York Minster following the disastrous fire there, started by Jonathan Martin, the previous February.

What was to become Wakefield's premier social event, the annual Charity Ball, owed its origin to the opening of the Music Saloon and perhaps also to the Reverend Martin Naylor, who wrote in 1827 in an editorial in *The Wakefield and Halifax Journal* of the dire need for funds for the Wakefield Dispensary and suggested the problem might be alleviated by the holding of a ball. The first took place on 9 April 1828 and was advertised as in aid of both the Dispensary and the House of Recovery. Towards the end of the century, the support of the gentry had gone, attendances became sparse and the one on 4 January 1899 was the last.

The saloon of the Corn Exchange in Westgate, built in 1838, rapidly overtook the Music Saloon as a premier place for entertainment as well as for public meetings. Solo performers, ensembles and even full-scale operas found a home there. The Charity Ball moved there in 1841.

Letting the Music Saloon, however, seems to have been vital to the income of the Mechanics Institution, which owned the Public Buildings from 1855. It was said in 1876 that the excellent tutor of the French class could not make himself heard above the noise of the violins from the dance floor.

Balls, simply as social entertainment and not necessarily for charities, grew in popularity especially in the later part of the century, and were put on by people of both the middle and working class. In the winter season of 1889-90, for example, there were balls, either in the Corn Exchange or the Music Saloon, for Wakefield Trinity Football Club, Wakefield butchers, Wakefield cyclists, post-office workers, Lancashire and Yorkshire Railway workers, George Lee's workpeople, the Yeomanry Cavalry, the Oddfellows, the Foresters, and the Wakefield Dr Primrose Habitation of the Primrose League. In 1888 the butchers decorated the dance hall with the heads or horns of slaughtered beasts! Wakefield Cricket Club had its first ball in February 1895.

Following the advent of rail travel in the 1840s, individual entertainers of national standing appeared in the Music Saloon from time to time. Henry Russell (1812-1900) who was both a composer and singer and whose 'Emigrant's Progress' is said to have spurred emigration to America, appeared in May 1845. George Grossmith read 'Pickings from Pickwick' in November 1849.

Charles Dickens read *A Christmas Carol* at the Corn Exchange in September 1858.

A room in what had formerly been the mansion of one of Wakefield's merchant princes, John Milnes, in Westgate, provided another venue for entertainment, including balls, from *c*1815 until 1840. A travelling museum, with 1,300 'natural curiosities', together with antiques and paintings, was housed there in August 1815. Admission was 1s. Servants and children were admitted at half price. In the 1830s the room was run by dancing-teacher Edward Willis, and became known simply as Willis's Rooms. In June 1838 the coronation of Queen Victoria was marked by a ball there and there was a ball in aid of the House of Recovery two months later. The property was sold later in 1838 although there was an exhibition of mechanical figures entitled, E Wigglesworth's Theatre of Arts, there in January 1839.

The short-lived Brears Concert Room, advertised as capable of holding 400 people, opened in the York Hotel Yard in February 1850 engaging local musicians and offering 'temperance refreshments'. It also provided the somewhat risque 'poses plastiques'.

Bazaars, providing another style of social gathering, were a favourite and frequent form of fund-raising and were, from its opening in 1838, normally held in the saloon of the Corn Exchange, often taking place over three or four days. Shortly before the Exchange was completed, a bazaar in aid of building a parsonage for Thornes Church was held in the Music Saloon in September 1838. In January 1840 a bazaar at the Corn Exchange raised funds for the Northern Congregational School at Silcoates. Possibly the most prestigious of all nineteenth century bazaars was that held in the Corn Exchange over a three-day period in July 1893. It was in aid of the Church of England Waifs and Strays Society and, more particularly, the Bede Home for boys in College Grove Road, Wakefield. On the first day the Archbishop of York, Walter Dalrymple, preached in Wakefield Cathedral before the bazaar was opened by Princess Christian, a daughter of Queen Victoria. The princess came to Wakefield as a guest of the bishop, William Walsham How, who had first met her when he was Bishop of Bedford. She stayed at Bishopgarth. The second day's opening ceremony was performed by Lady Beatrice Lister Kaye, and the third day saw the Duchess of Devonshire undertake the opening.

Circuses and other visiting shows

Equestrian shows and circuses visited Wakefield perennially, sometimes at the time of the summer or autumn fairs. It has not proved possible to establish when the first came, however Wild's 'New Riding School' was set up in King Street for the July fair in 1805 whilst Kite and Moritz's Circus was to be found at the same time further up King Street. The New Olympic Circus was sited in Wood Street in July 1812 with entertainment that was largely equestrian but included rope dancing; there were three classes of admission, at two shillings, one shilling and sixpence, and a shilling. Cooke's Olympic Circus performed in the yard of the *Woodman Inn* in Wood Street in 1821 and returned regularly thereafter. In 1842 the Amercan Circus set up in Pitchforth's field at the bottom of York Street. Pablo Fanque's circus spent some weeks in Wood Street in the winter of 1846-7.

The fairs attracted other side-shows besides portable theatres. In 1849, for example, there were stalls for sweets and 'spice meats', a wax-work display, and Punch and Judy.

Mr Hathaway's 'Cabinet of Wax Figures' was exhibited in June 1812 in 'committee rooms' in Northgate. The figures were said to be life size and represented members of the British Royal family and the tragic French royal family. There was also a representation of Nelson's funeral. Admission cost a shilling.

Madame Tussaud (1760-1850) brought life-size wax figures to the Crown Court Assembly Rooms in March 1820. Another collection of waxworks was exhibited in ten caravans in 1832.

Wombwell's Menagerie visited the town on a number of occasions, what was probably the first time at Christmas 1831. George Wombwell (1777-1850) had begun showing wild animals in premises in Soho but in 1810 he began travelling with brightly coloured wagons displaying jungle scenes and containing wildcats, wolves, monkeys, giraffes, elephants and camels.

Before the advent of motion pictures at the end of the century, visual entertainment came to Wakefield in the form of panoramas. These involved enormous lengths of painted canvas moved by means of giant rollers. They portrayed either significant events or impressive scenes from around the world. The idea is attributed to an eighteenth century Scottish painter, Robert Barker, who first exhibited one in England in Leicester Square in 1792. In some towns and cities rotundas were created to display them. Elsewhere, as in Wakefield, they were either shown in whatever halls were available or in *ad hoc* temporary structures. When the first of these came to Wakefield is not clear but it may have been in 1814 when William Sinclair brought panoramas of the Battle of Trafalgar and the more-recent Coronation of George IV to the White Hart Assembly Rooms in August 1822. Admission was 2s, 1s, or, if you were prepared to stand throughout the exhibition, 6d. In later years panoramas were housed in the Music Saloon, the Corn Exchange, or Willis's Rooms. Laidlaw's Panorama was exhibited in April 1840 in the Music Saloon. It included scenes in Jerusalem, images of Sir John Ross's voyage and pictures of the coronation of Queen Victoria. In 1842 a pavilion was set up in Wood Street for a Mrs Hunter's panorama of Damascus. A panorama of the 1848 murder at Stanfield Hall, Norfolk, was set up again in a pavilion in Wood Street in 1849.

Despite the visiting panoramas and the impact of *The Illustrated London News* from 1842, there was comparatively little access to visual images in the nineteenth century. A seemingly popular treat was the exhibition of a supposedly instructional 'history' painting, taken on tour. Francis Danby's 1828 apocalyptic painting of the opening of the Sixth Seal, for example,was exhibited in April 1840 in the Corn Exchange for a substantial admission price of a shilling with a reduction for working people and children to 6d. There were many more similar occasions.

Two skilled amateur artists painted Wakefield scenes in the nineteenth century, sometimes providing a valuable historical record where no other image exists. Louisa Fennell (1847-1930) the daughter of a Wakefield wine merchant, studied under John Battye Tootal at the Wakefield School of Art, and under Thomas Hartley Cromek (1809-1873) who spent his later years in Wakefield. Thomas Kilby (1794-1868), who was the vicar of St John's Church from 1825 until his death in 1868 produced *Scenery in the Vicinity of Wakefield by an amateur* in 1843.

Excursions

The railways provided a chance for the ordinary people to see rather more of the country. Some 2000 Oddfellows and friends left Wakefield in a train drawing thirty-one carriages for a day trip to Liverpool in August 1844. The following July a special train of fifty carriages took them for a weekend in Scarborough. Their return journey allowed for a two-hour stop in York to see the Minster or its other sights.

Possibly the first attractive opportunity for Wakefield people to visit London came on 8 April 1850 when a J Calverley of South Street, Primrose Hill and a Mr Cuttle arranged an excursion train from Normanton to Euston. Wakefield people could board it at Oakenshaw Station. The return trip cost 32s first class or 20s in a 'covered waggon'.

The Great Northern Railway advertised the opportunity for a week's stay in London in September 1850 with return fares to King's Cross Station varying from 35s 6d for first-class travel to 16s 2d for a third-class seat. In 1851 the Midland and the Great Northern Railways vied to take parties of Wakefield people to the Great Exhibition which opened at the Crystal Palace on 1 May. The return fare was 5s. The Mechanics Institution formed a club for savings and subscriptions towards paying for its members to attend the exhibition.

Cheap Trip to Liverpool.

The Public are respectfully informed that
On *MONDAY, SEPTEMBER 8th,* 1845,
A Cheap Trip will take place from

WAKEFIELD TO LIVERPOOL
AND BACK

TO leave the Wakefield Station at Five o'Clock in the Morning, and return from Liverpool at Seven in the Evening of the same day, allowing full TEN HOURS for the Party to remain in Liverpool.

FARES:—

Third Class, there and back,   4s. 0d.
Second Class,   Do.   6s. 6d.
First Class,   Do.   8s. 6d.

The Committee feel confident that this will be a favourable opportunity for all persons who wish to see Liverpool;—and as the season is so far advanced, it is very probable that another opportunity will not be offered to them.

The Committee also beg to state that they are making arrangements with the Proprietors of the ZOOLOGICAL GARDENS (Which are said to be the finest and best conducted of the kind in Great Britain,) at a very reduced rate.

TICKETS for the TRIP may be had of any of the Committee; at the Railway Station; of the following persons, viz:—Mr. Robinson, Bookseller, Kirkgate; Mr. Wm. Wroe, Provision Dealer, Wrengate; Mr. G. Rathmell, Hair Dresser, top of Westgate; Mr. Roberts, Hair Dresser, opposite the Church; Mr. Green, Provision Dealer, Northgate; Mr. G. Milthorp, Public Baths, Wood Street; Mr. J. Hewitt, Hair Dresser, Westgate; Mr. Garforte, Grocer, Westgate; Mr. Scarth, Corn and Provision Dealer, Westgate Common; Mr James Widdop, Hair Dresser, Barstow-square; and at the *Journal Office.*

Figure 86: An advertisement for railway excursions. *Yorkshire Archaeological Society*

Brass band competitions were fostered by railway travel. The first 'modern' brass band was probably that founded in Stalybridge in 1814. A Wakefield Band was formed in 1843. From the 1850s numerous works and colliery brass bands were founded. In Wakefield, the Rutland Mills Band was, perhaps, the most popular and longest surviving. The first band competition was held at Belle Vue, Manchester, in 1851. Brass bands went to the south with the first of the competitions at Crystal Palace in July 1860. Excursion trains ran from Wakefield and Pontefract for a three-night stay in the capital.

Open space, commercial gardens, recreation grounds and a public park
In the mid-eighteenth century, fashionable Wakefield people enjoyed the delights of the Strafford Gardens, Wakefield's Vauxhall, in Northgate. It was not until the 1830s that commercial gardens were again provided. The first were Barratt's subscription gardens, covering three acres on the east side of Margaret Street and opened in 1833. Later that year they were described as one of the principal attractions for visitors to the town. The proprietor, William Baratt, had begun as a nurseryman and seed-merchant. Subscribers to the gardens – and by 1834 there were 200 of them – were able to buy plants to the value of their subscriptions. Sometimes a band was engaged to play in the evenings. In 1836 Barratt added a conservatory and greenhouses and had plans for a library of books and journals on gardening. The gardens were featured in the issue of *The Gardeners' Magazine* in June 1836 (Figure 87). The gardens were still a major attraction in 1862 when

Figure 87: Drawing of Barratt's hothouses from the *Gardening Magazine*. *The John Goodchild Collection*

the band of Wakefield Rifle Corps put on concerts there on Thursday evenings throughout the summer. Barrett's house and land were sold in May 1867 and the sale of the vineries, greenhouses etc followed in August.

In October 1838, *The Wakefield Herald* carried a large advertisement promoting the Botanical and Zoological Gardens which were to be established in Back Lane in what had been the Orangery for Pemberton House in Westgate. Wakefield people could enjoy the facility for an annual individual subscription of 10s 6d or for a family subscriptionof £1 10s 6d. In 1837 a swimming bath was added to the attractions.

For poorer people, Heath Common must have been a welcome place of recreation (Figure 88). Sporting events took place there, including numerous Knurr and Spell matches, and the Volunteers and Yeomanry Cavalry used it for exercise. In 1844, however, it came under threat. John George Smyth, the lord of the Manor of Warmfield and Heath, proposed bringing a bill to Parliament for its inclosure. This would have resulted in its being apportioned out amongst those with common rights and then developed either for agriculture or even housing. Leading Wakefield figures, and some tenants of the mansions at Heath, were opposed to the scheme as was the Barnsley Canal Company whose waterway lay for a distance beside it. Charles Waterton issued placards aiming to rouse public concern. There was a public meeting and petition to Parliament was drawn up claiming that the Common was the only 'lung' for Wakefield's 15,000 inhabitants, many of whom were 'engaged in trade and manufactories'. More compellingly the petition pointed out that earlier legislation had recognised that no commons should be inclosed where they lay within a mile and a half of a town of over 1,500 people. Heath Common, it was noted, was just that distance from the Wakefield's central market place. The bill was lost.

Wealthy mill owners and others living in or near Wakefield had large houses and grounds, worked by head and assistant gardeners. In the 1870s the gardeners were in the habit of meeting together at the *Saw Inn* in Little Westgate where the landlord, Councillor A Lupton, was ready to give them a private room. In 1877 the group was established on a more formal footing as the Wakefield Paxton Society with J P Carter, J Henshall and T Garnett as its founders. Their objects were to hand on a knowledge of gardening, to exhibit flowers and plants and to form a library. Lupton was appointed as the first curator. A charge of 2s 6d was made for joining the Society and there was an annual subscription of a further 2s 6d. It was at a meeting in 1886 that a scheme was mooted to provide Wakefield with a public park. The following year the Society suggested that a public park would be an excellent means of marking Queen Victoria's golden jubilee. Many years earlier, Jose Luis Fernandes had suggested that Lawe Hill might best be utilised as a public park. Nothing came of the idea initially, however the desirability of open spaces became accepted. The Society opened a recreation ground in Pinderfields Road in September 1889. The generosity of Richard Holdsworth and Mrs Fred Thompson led to another ground being opened in

Figure 88: Heath Common where it is just possible to discern that cricket is being played.
The John Goodchild Collection

Ings Road. In March 1890 a three-acre recreation ground, provided by Edith Mackie, opened on Balne Lane; the area was divided with boys separated from girls. Again in 1890 Charles George Milnes Gaskell offered two acres from his Thornes House estate at Lawe Hill to the Paxton Society with the prospect of buying further land at a modest price. The Duke of Clarence and Avondale visited the site of the proposed park on 30 April 1891 and planted a white horse chestnut. The area was laid out with paths, shelters at either end of the 'east' walk, a lodge at the Park Road entrance, and a bandstand on Lawe Hill. The main avenue was planted with a double row of 108 chestnuts many of which still stand

Figure 89: The main avenue of horse chestnuts at Clarence Park. *The author*

Figure 90: Sandal Castle in the 1880s. *Yorkshire Archaeological Society*

more than 100 years later (Figure 89). The park was opened on 6 July 1893, the day of the marriage of the Duke of York and Princess May. On the same day, and in particular because of his service to the public-park movement, Charles George Milnes Gaskell was given the freedom of the city. For five years trustees of the Wakefield Public Park Maintenance Fund managed the park but in 1898 it was conveyed to Wakefield Corporation.

Sandal Castle and its grounds were given to Sandal Local Board in 1889 by the Pilkington family as a recreation ground (Figure 90).

Clubs and societies

Many of the clubs and societies founded in Wakefield, and more especially from the 1830s onwards, were probably quite short lived. There were various choral societies, some promoted by individual places of worship. A Wakefield Choral

Society was formed by 1832. An Amateur Musical Society gave concerts in the 1830s.

The parish church had its Society of Change Ringers, first established in 1796, which undertook marathon ringing. In October 1821 for example, a team of nine, led by William Woodhead, rang 5,079 changes in three hours and eleven minutes. The complex figure was described as Caters on Stedman principal. Wakefield & District Organists Association was formed in 1889/90 to promote the organ and its music within its own ranks, and the general public and to provide a 'fellowship of organists'. It is the world's first and therefore oldest Organists' Association. It was instrumental in forming the Incorporated Association of Organists in 1911. Jeremiah Dunnill was an early member; he was President in 1896.

The West Riding Horticultural Society, based originally in Wakefield, was formed in the 1830s when it held shows of fruits, flowers and vegetables in the hall of the Proprietory School. One of the earliest of the floral societies to be formed in the area was the Royal Oak Florists' Club which was active in the 1840s. The longest surviving and best known Wakefield society was the Tulip Society, founded in 1835 or 1838 and later expanded as the Wakefield and North of England Tulip Society.

Wakefield's Agricultural and Horticultural shows originated in 1862 when a Floral Exhibition on 4 September, principally of dahlias, took place in a field lying between Ings Road and Denby Dale Road close to the great railway viaduct. It was, explicitly, the successor to Bretton's Flower Shows and was masterminded by Wakefield solicitor, Joseph Wainwright. It became an annual event extending to livestock in 1865. By 1868 a gymkhana had been added and special trains were being run to Wakefield to bring people seeking a day out. That occasion was marred, however, when the 'grandstand' collapsed and several people suffered fractures. The following year the show moved to a field in the Borough Market area and was, for the first time, a two-day event.

Wakefield Farmers' Club was described in 1842 as 'lately established'. It met at the *Great Bull Inn* or at the *George Hotel* for dinners and to hear papers on agricultural topics such as 'The harvesting and housing of corn' or on 'Mechanical Drills'.

Following the promotion of a bill in Parliament, supported by Wakefield MP Daniel Gaskell, and his nephew James Milnes Gaskell, MP for Much Wenlock, the Wakefield branch of the SPCA (later the RSPCA) was founded in 1836. The first meeting, in the Court House on 28 April, brought together Wakefield worthies of all complexions. The committee included Reverend Samuel Sharp, Reverend W T Alderson who was then the chaplain at the prison, the Unitarian minister Reverend Thomas Johnstone, and another staunch dissenter, Caleb Crowther. The Society provided a horse trough at the bottom of Westgate, as a tribute to Ann Clarkson, in August 1888. (It was moved in the twentieth century to Clarence Park.)

Figure 91: Wakefield Masonic Hall in 2007. *The author*

The first Lodge of Freemasons to be established in Wakefield, Unanimity, had been founded in 1765 and for most of the nineteenth century held its meetings at the *Bull Hotel*. Wakefield Lodge was founded in 1844, meeting in Thornhill Street, and the Lodge of Sincerity came into being twenty years later, in 1864. Much of the Rectory House was pulled down by the Borough Market Company but Wakefield Lodge bought what remained in 1853, for a Masonic Hall. Other Lodges joined them and a new building was erected on the site in 1880-81 (Figure 91). Zetland Street, which it fronts, was named after the Earl of Zetland who was Grand Master of the English Freemasons from 1844 to 1870.

There were numerous, and sometimes short-lived, cricket clubs, often playing their matches on Heath Common. *The Wakefield Examiner* commented in 1850 on the problem in forming any permanent cricket club because the necessary young men were 'a moving body'. Both the Mechanics Institution and the Church Institution had clubs. The most permanent were Wakefield Cricket Club which was formed in 1870, acquiring a ground in 1872 in College Grove Road from John G Smirthwaite, who provided a pavilion designed by William Crutchley, and St Michael's Cricket Club which has survived into the twenty-first century with its field in Dewsbury Road and which began in the 1890s as the St Michael's Youth Football and Cricket Club. The cricket club at Hodgson and Simpson's Calder Soap Works was formed in 1880 and brought in a Yorkshire county player, Andrew Greenwood, to coach its members.

By 1880, cricket in the area was so popular that in the summer months *The Wakefield Express* had a full column devoted to match results. There were clubs in the surrounding villages, attached to churches, or formed at the workplace.

Much the most important of Wakefield's sports clubs was, and is, Wakefield Trinity Football Club, known in the twenty-first century as Wakefield Wildcats. It began, as its name suggests, at Holy Trinity Church in George Street and was founded in 1873 by the Young Men's Society there, with the support of a Wakefield lawyer, John H Dixon. It played the amateur Rugby Union rather than the later League game. Some of its earliest matches took place at Heath Common and then on fields near the *Alexandra Hotel* at Belle Vue. The Club became independent of the church in 1884, moving its meeting room from the parochial rooms to Holly Lodge in Lord Rodney Yard. In 1892 the club leased, and then bought, its permanent site near to St Catherine's Church at Belle Vue. A problem faced the Club in that its players were working men who had to take unpaid leave from work to train and play. The Rugby Union resisted the professional status that wages would have implied. At first Wakefield, and other similar northern clubs, broke away from the national union and formed the Northern Rugby Union. This developed into the National Rugby League in 1895 with sides of thirteen men rather than the Union's fifteen.

Numerous other organisations included Wakefield Anglers' Club which was founded in 1845, the Naturalists' Society which was in existence by 1862, and Wakefield Cycling Club which was formed in the 1880s.

Wakefield regattas and races

A group of 'respectable gentlemen' planned in 1848 to establish an annual regatta on the Calder. Their first – and perhaps last – event took place in September 1850 drawing competitors from Chester, Manchester and Worcester as well as locally. The bells were rung in the parish church, flags flew from many buildings, the riverside was dotted with marquees and Wakefield shops and businesses took a holiday. The Regatta course was from the woodland at Heath to Fall Ing Lock (Figure 92). A problem for the competitors was the steady stream of working vessels using the waterway.

The Wakefield Amateur Rowing Association, which had been founded at a meeting at the *Jolly Sailor Inn* on 13 October 1868 following a successful race between Wakefield and Leeds crews on the Calder in August 1867, held its first Regatta on 7 August 1869. The new course was west of Wakefield along the River Calder beside Daniel Gaskell's parkland at Lupset Hall. The band of Wakefield's Rifle Corps was enlisted to entertain the crowds which included inmates from the Asylum. Although the enclosure and refreshment tent, erected close to the

Figure 92: The stretch of river used for Wakefield's first regatta. *The author*

winning post, were patronised by Wakefield's leading figures (including Major Joseph Barker, C E M Gaskell, W H Gill, W S Banks, the Reverend Goodwyn Barmby), it was not by any means a success. Some of the races had to be scratched for lack of competitors. And it poured with rain. Despite this poor beginning, the Rowing Club held further regattas in the 1870s. By 1873 the Regatta was a two-day event with races on land as well as by water. The Regatta of 1875 was the most successful yet. It took place on 10 July again close to Lupset Hall. Special trains were put on to Wakefield, and all the trains on the Lancashire and Yorkshire Railway stopped at Horbury Junction. The Buccleuch, Burton on Trent, Derwent, Middlesbrough and York amateur rowing clubs joined teams from Wakefield and umpiring was in the judgment of men from the Cambridge Union Boat Club. Trophies included the Corporation Plate, Heath Plate, Tradesmen's Plate and the Wakefield Challenge Cup. It was estimated that some

8,000 spectators lined the river. *The Wakefield Express* noted that 'the stench which usually arises from the Calder was all but imperceptible, the recent freshes having cleansed it of some of its impurities'. Entertainment was provided by Captain Paul Boyton who had achieved fame, or notoriety, by swimming the Channel in an inflatable life jacket. However, because of the death of Daniel Gaskell, there was no regatta in 1876, with the Wakefield Rowing Club instead holding a series of competitive events during the summer in the stretch of river between the *Jolly Sailor* and the Hodgson and Simpson's soap works at Thornes. No record of further regattas has yet been found.

There was other boating on the Calder. Pleasure boats were for a period available for hire from Mounseer's on Stennard Island. Favourite trips were to the Cheesecake Shop at Kirkthorpe or to the chain bridge where the turnpike to Denby Dale crossed the river.

Wakefield Races had ceased in 1794. However there was a short-lived revival of racing locally when a Wakefield Steeplechase was got up in 1847 with horses jumping ditches and hedges in the Durkar area. This developed into the Crigglestone Races, held annually over two days in the early 1850s.

Public baths

Following a public meeting in March 1832 and the inevitable request for subscriptions, public baths were established in the basement of the Wood Street Public Buildings the following September, taking the place of the Wakefield Dispensary and, no doubt, designed to replace the lost income from the Dispensary's rent. Amongst the promoters was Wakefield's vicar Samuel Sharp. Whilst the baths very possibly had a recreational element, families could attend together for 10s 6d; they were provided primarily for hygienic or medicinal purposes. They included a vapour, or steam, bath, a warm bath, a plunge bath and a shower.

In the late 1860s and early 1870s there were moves to persuade the Council to build swimming baths but the idea was rejected on the grounds of cost. The baths were built in Almshouse Lane by a company established in 1873, following an initiative by the Trinity Church Young Men's Society and a public meeting – crowded it was reported by young working-class men – in the Corn Exchange in August. The baths opened in 1874. The opening of the baths led to Wakefield Swimming Club's being founded at a public meeting at the *Strafford Arms Hotel* on 5 October 1875. It held its first gala the following July.

During the winter months of 1875-6, the swimming pool was, for the first time, floored over and was opened for roller skating. Music was provided by Jeremiah Dunnill's band or by a pianist. So popular was the activity that the Wakefield Skating Rink Company was formed by J A Coates in May 1876 to establish a purpose-built all-year rink in Coates Terrace, Kirkgate, but the scheme came to nothing. It was not until 1909 that Wakefield got the Olympia Rink in Ings Road. The Almshouse Lane baths were taken over by Wakefield Corporation in 1884.

Wakefield en fete

Wakefield people enjoyed many opportunities for public celebrations, some of them unusual if not unique. Three might be noted here. In July 1820, following a requisition to the Constable, possibly prompted by the radical clergyman Martin Naylor, a meeting of townspeople resolved unanimously to send a 'dutiful and loyal' address to Queen Caroline. When the bill to strip her of her title and end her marriage to George IV was abandoned by Parliament in November, a triumphal arch was erected at Lupset Hall, there were fireworks at Hatfeild Hall and coloured lamps in the trees at Stanley Hall. The church bells rang, sheep were roasted, and buildings were illuminated.

The Festival of Bishop Blaise, patron saint of woolcombers, was revived by a group of Wakefield woolcombers and woolsorters in February 1829 after a gap, it was said, of thirty-five years. The procession, which wound its way from 10am to 4pm, began at Westgate Common, took a circuitous route through town to St John's, and then progressed to Heath, returning via Belle Isle. At the heart of the procession was 'Bishop Blaise' with his 'chaplain' followed by a shepherd with a lamb. The event raised £6 for Wakefield Dispensary but was never repeated.

Figure 93: The prison entrance in Love Lane. *Yorkshire Archaeological Society*

Queen Victoria never visited Wakefield but in September 1858 she was carried by train through the town on her way to Leeds where she opened the new Town Hall. Wakefield could not miss the chance to celebrate her passing. Buildings that could be seen from the train were decorated with flags and bunting. The entrance to the prison, in Love Lane, and the flanking houses of the Governor and Chaplain, were hung with evergreens and flowers (Figure 93). Crowds packed Kirkgate Station. A cannon, which was a trophy from the battle of Sebastopol, was taken to a field in Ings Road, and fired as the Queen passed by.

Sources

Kate Taylor, *Right Royal, Wakefield Theatre 1776-1994*, 1995.
Sam Wild, *Old Wild's: A nursery of strolling players*, 1888.
Percy A Scholes, *The Concise Oxford Dictionary of Music*, 1952.
The petition to Parliament opposing the inclosure of Heath Common. *The John Goodchild Collection*
L Shaw, *A short history of Wakefield Paxton Society 1877-1967*.
John Goodchild, *The Masonic Hall, Zetland Street, Wakefield*, 1996.
C Lindley, *100 Years of Rugby: The History of Wakefield Trinity 1873-1973*, 1973.

Bibliography

principal sources used throughout the book.

W S Banks, *Walks about Wakefield*, 1871
Henry Clarkson, *Memories of Merry Wakefield: An Octogenarian's Recollection, 1801-1887*, 1887
John Hewitt, *The History and Topography of the Parish of Wakefield and its Environs*, 1862
Kate Taylor, ed, *Wakefield District Heritage*, 1976
Kate Taylor, ed, *Wakefield District Heritage* (Volume II), 1979
Kate Taylor, ed, *Worthies of Wakefield*, 2004
J W Walker, *Wakefield, its History and its People*, Wakefield, 1939
Street Commissioners' Minute Books
Wakefield Corporation Minute Books
West Riding Quarter Sessions Order Books
Local newspapers
Trade directories

Other titles in the Series

The Making of Barnsley, Brian Elliott
The Making of Huddersfield, George Redmonds
The Making of the South Yorkshire Landscape, Melvyn Jones
The Making of Leeds, David Goodman
The Making of Sheffield, Melvyn Jones
The Making of Shrewsbury, Vivien Bellamy
The Making of the West Yorkshire Landscape, Anthony Silson
The Making of Wigan, Mike Fletcher

$\mathcal{I}$NDEX

Agricultural shows 166
Ainley, Mary 138
Aire and Calder Navigation 70, 80, 81
Aire and Calder waggonway 80, 81
Albion works 94
Alder, Thomas 23
Alderson, W T 166
Aldred, Ebenezer 84
Alhambra 152
Almshouses 51-2
Altree, J 138
Alverthorpe Hall 139
Amateur theatricals 152
Andrews and Delaney 111
Antonio, 'Baron' 153
Aqueduct, Stanley Ferry 71
Armytage, Charlotte 54
Arnold, Mr 64
Aspdin, Joseph 74, 91
Assembly rooms 66, 98, 99, 102, 143, 147, 159
Assizes 21, 30, 34, 39, 64, 66, 115
Atkinson and Sharp 104, 157
Atkinson, George 152
Avison, Thomas 39
Bakewell, William 43
Band of Hope 137
Banks, James 147
Banks, W S 31, 74, 91, 169
Banks and Building Societies
  Barclays 77
  Beckett and Co 77
  HSBC 80
  Ingram, Kennett and Ingram 76-7
  Leatham and Tew 77, 78-79
  Leeds and County 80
  Midland 80
  Penny 137
  Post Office 77
  Shackleton 76
  Townend and Rishworth 76
  Wakefield and Barnsley Union 77
  Wakefield Banking Co 77
  Wakefield and West Riding Building Society 80
  Wakefield Building Society 77
  Wakefield Savings Bank 77
  Wentworth and Chaloner 76
  Wentworth, Chaloner and Rishworth 76
  York City and County 80
  Yorkshire Penny 77
Bank House 77
Barber, Swinden 54
Barff, John 26, 39, 151
Barker and Co 85
Barker, Joseph 52, 111, 117, 134, 169
Barker, Robert 159
Barmby, Goodwyn 113, 169
Barnsley Canal 71
Barnsley Canal Co 162
Barratt, Robert 140
Barratt, William 131, 161
Barratt's gardens 161
Barstow, Charles 29
Baths 170

Bauwen, L F 94
Bayldon, Jonathan 29
Beaumont, Somerset 40
Bede Home 119, 158
Bell, Andrew 129
Bennett, Philip 35
Berry, John Wood 24
Bigland, John 89
Bilberry reservoir 26, 114
Billinton, William 87
Bishopgarth 119
Blanchard, Edwin 153
Board of Guardians 4, 7, 23, 27, 47-50, 52, 62, 88
Boat building 72
Bolland, Thomas 17
Booth, General 103
Booth, John Samuel 86
Botanical gardens 162
Bourne, Hugh 99
Bowditch, William 109, 112-3, 129, 130
Boyton, Paul 170
Bradley and Craven 92
Bradley, George 19
Bradley, Richard 92, 96
Bramah, Joseph 67
Brass bands 160-2
Brears Concert Rooms 158
Bretton Hall 40
Breweries
  Beverleys 92
  Crown 92
  Melbourne 92
  Old Bridge 92
  Phoenix 92
  Victoria 92
Brick-making 70
Brierley, John 21
Briggs, Elizabeth 29
Briggs, Isaac 29
Briggs, Isaac and Son 85-6
Briggs, John 134
British Ropes 80
Broadhead, Thomas 31
Bromley, John 126
Brooke, Joseph 140
Brotherton, E A 92, 94
Browne, James Crichton 48
Burden, J 138
Butterton, G A 123
Calder and Hebble Navigation 71, 80
Calverley, J 160
Cameron, John
Camidge, Charles J, 55
Camin, 'Baron' de 112
Carlton House 56
Caroline, Queen 171
Carpenter, William Boyd 119
Carr, John 98
Carr, Walter 66
Carter, H M 153
Carter, J P 92, 162
Carter, Thomas 92
Carter, William 39
Catalani, Angelica 55
Cattle Dealers and Graziers Association 90

Chald House 54
Cemetery 56-7
Chamber of Commerce 62
Chamber of Trade 62
Change ringing 126, 166
Chapels and Churches
  All Saints (Wakefield parish church, cathedral) 5, 57, 62, 97, 106, 115-6, 124-6, 145, 157
  Baptist 56, 111, 103, 139
  Belle Vue 100
  Bethel 100
  Brunswick 100
  Chantry 107-8
  Chapel of the Destitute 137
  Christ Church 110, 111
  Christian 103
  Christian Israelites 103
  Eastmoor 99, 111
  Ebenezer 99, 116-7
  Flanshaw 101
  Grove Road 100
  Holy Trinity 55, 016, 168, 110, 112, 116, 118
  John Street 101
  New Scarborough 99
  Newmillerdam 100
  Quebec Street 100, 102
  St Andrew's 56, 109, 112, 113
  St Austin's 116, 111
  St Catherine's 109, 117
  St Faith's 109
  St Helen's 98, 109, 113, 115, 156
  St James's 56-7, 103, 115, 117, 158
  St John's 56, 97, 106, 111, 115, 118, 125
  St Mark's 109
  St Mary's 108, 109, 113
  St Michael's 109, 110, 112
  St Paul's 103, 104, 105, 115
  St Peter's 103, 112
  St Peter and St Leonard's 98, 115
  Salem 56, 98, 99, 100, 127, 138
  Society of Friends (Quakers) 56, 98, 99,
  Spiritualist 10
  United Free Methodist 100, 103
  Westgate Chapel (Unitarian) 56, 98, 117, 133, 139
  Westgate End 99
  West Parade 62, 98, 99, 103, 117, 118, 131
  Zion 98 101, 113
Chapman, Ronald 122
Charity balls 45, 157
Charlesworth, C E 153
Charlesworth, John Barff 39
Charlesworth, J C D 39
Charnock, J H 70
Chartists 18, 143
Chipstead, James Aubrey 27
Cholera 46-7, 55, 124
Christian, Princess 158
Church Congress 117
Church Institute 62, 68, 80, 118, 145
Church Institution 119, 143, 145, 167

Church Missionary Society 115
Church rate 65-6, 115
Circuses
    American 159
    Cooke's Olympic 155, 158-9
    Fanque's 159
    Kite and Moritz's 159
    People's Empire 153, 155
Clapham, Charles 109
Clarence, Duke of 145, 163
Clarence Park 54, 162, 166
Clarke, Cornelius 138
Clarkson, Ann 54, 166
Clarkson, Henry 15, 17, 48, 68, 70, 138
Clarkson, John 84
Clarkson, William 29
Clay, Charles 92
Clayton, Thomas 43
Coalmining 70, 76, 80
Coates, J A 170
Cobbe, Charles, 23
Cocoa and coffee taverns 124
Colcutt, T E 31
Collieries
    Ackton Hall 20
    Balne Lane, 82
    California 82
    Cookson and Co 80
    Denby Grange 80
    Fenton's 80
    Fernandes, Dunn and Walker 81
    Hudson and Co 82
    Lupset 80
    Manor 80
    Middleton 152
    New Victoria 35
    Park Hill 81, 141
    Providence 82
    Roundwood 82
    St John's Grove 80
    Sharlston 45
    Smithson's 80
    Victoria Coal Co 81
    Wath Main 60
    Westgate Common 80
    Whinney Moor 80
Collins, Oliver Levey 106
Comerford, James 154
Connor, John 140
Conservative Association 39, 67
Cooke, George 137
Cooper, Robert 140
Cope, Richard 100, 101, 139
Corn Exchange 54, 62, 87, 88, 100,
    113, 117, 145, 154, 157-160
Corn Trade committee 87
Couldery, William 60
County Hall 41, 62
Court House 10, 11, 23, 29, 31, 39,
    60, 88, 104, 111, 115, 143, 156, 166
Coxley Valley 43
Cradock, George 80, 94
Craven, George 24, 115
Cricket 167
Cromek, Thomas H 139, 160
Cr_oueste, Edward 154
Crowther, Caleb 46, 51, 166
Crutchley, William 94, 167
Crystal Palace 161
Cussons, John 64
Cuttle, Mr 160
Dalrymple, Walter 158
Dalton, Francis 21

Danby, Francis 159
Davies, Charles G 106
Davies and Tew 134
Dawson, William 46
Dear, James 133
Devonshire, Duchess of 158
Diamond Coal-Cutting Co 92
Dickens, Charles 158
Dioceses
    Ripon 97, 118
    Wakefield 97, 118
    York 97
Dixon, Benjamin 111
Dixon, John H 168
Dixon, Marion 24
Doyle, Thomas 19
Drill Hall 19, 117
Dunn, Richard 34, 81, 84
Dunnill, Jeremiah 170
Dykes, John Bacchus 107, 123
Dykes, Thomas 107
Dykes, William 109, 145
Dykes, William Hey 107, 109
Dyeworks
    Calder 92
    Belle Isle (Holdsworth's) 39. 67, 84
    Halliley and Co 84
Eastmead, John S 55, 140, 141
Ebenezer Glass Bottle works 92
Edwards, J P 153
Electricity 51, 61
Ellis, Amon 146
Fairs 28, 91, 130, 147, 153, 158
Fallon and Watmough 85
Farnell, H B 49-50
Fawcett, George 141
Fawcett, James 35, 131
Featherstone disaster 20
Fenians 19
Fennell, E E 54
Fennell, Louisa 140, 160
Fernandes, Jose Luis 35, 81, 84
Fernandes J L jun'r 35, 92, 162
Fernandes, Noel Luis 35, 92
Fire service 67
Fitzwilliam, Earl 16, 36
Fitch, Joshua G 126
Flatman, John 26
Flax 86
Flockton, J 138
Flockton, Thomas 24
Foster, Edward 139
Foster, James 17
Fothergill, John 101
France G H 31
Freemasonry 167
Friendly Societies 55, 157, 160
Garforth, William 92
Garnett, T 162
Gasgoigne T O 37
Gaskell, Benjamin 103
Gaskell, Catherine Milnes 54
Gaskell, Charles G M 42, 43, 163, 169
Gaskell, Daniel 36, 133, 135, 149, 166,
    168
Gaskell, James Milnes 37, 103, 166
Gaskell, Louisa Milnes 43
Geological and Polytechnic Society 143
Gibson, James 42
Gilbert, W S 48
Gill, Elizabeth 130
Gill, W H 169
Gissing, George 134

Godley, William 131
Goldthorpe, J and Co
Goldthorpe, Richard E 35
Governors of the Wakefield Charities
    51, 89, 108, 122, 125, 129
Great Exhibition 94, 160
Green, Edward 8, 94, 131
Green, Edward jun'r 40, 92, 94, 140,
    141, 145, 153
Green, George 115
Green, Mary 40, 141
Greenwood, Andrew 168
Grossmith, George 157
Grove House 114
Guild of Pity 54
Haigh Hall 106
Hall, William 23
Hall, William R 66
Halliley, T 54
Hamer, Mrs 54
Hansom, Joseph 116
Harcourt, Fred 155
Hardy, Thomas 120
Harewood, Earl of 36
Harrison, Enoch 138-9
Harrison, George W 8, 24, 27, 28,
    100, 131, 153
Harrison, Joseph 52
Harrison, Sarah 52
Harrison, Robert 92
Harrison, Samuel Fozzard 45, 52
Hartley, Bernard 73
Heath Common 16, 17, 23, 162, 167,
    171
Heath Hall 139
Heath Old Hall 153
Hebden, Will 155
Hemsworth Hall 39
Henshall, J 162
Hepworth, William 65
Hewell and Son 64
Hewitt, John 57, 76
Hey, Robert 146
Heywood, Arthur 149
Heywood, Benjamin 16
Heywood, John P 125, 127, 149
Heywood, Mrs 45
Higgins, Arthur 64
Higginson, Edward 139
Higham, Alfred B 145
Hill, William 100
Hodgson and Simpson 94, 111, 168
Hodgson, Robert 106
Hodgson, Thomas 43
Hodgson, W T
Holdsworth, James 24
Holdsworth, Joseph 39, 84
Holdsworth, Richard 162
Holdsworth, Samuel 84
Horbury Common Lands Trust 115
Horne, Cotton 51
Horne, William 51
Horner, Joseph 115
Horridge, George 85
Horsfall, William 17
Hospital Saturday 43
Hospital Sunday 43
Hospitals, dispensaries etc
    Carr Gate 52
    Clayton 43, 45
    Eye Dispensary 47
    Fever 52
    House of Recovery 45-47, 152, 157-8

Lupset Lodge 52
Wakefield Dispensary 43, 51, 152,
  155, 157, 170
West Riding Pauper Lunatic Asylum
  47, 60, 82, 109, 141
Houghton, Lord 54
House of Correction 10, 34, 138
House of Refuge (Industrial Home for
  Women) 54
How, William Walsham 109, 119, 120
Hubbarde, James Dibdin 65
Hudson, Robert 59, 82
Hurst, Rowland 64
Hurst, Rowland jun'r 65, 66
Illingworth, Mr 67
Irish, The 70, 112-3
Jackson, Joseph 83
Jackson's Arcade 95-6
Jaritt, Francis
Johnson, Joseph 29
Johnson, William 138
Johnstone, Thomas 139, 166
Jones, Henry 140
Jones, John 106
Kaye, Lady Beatrice Lister 158
Kilby, Thomas 160
Kilham, Alexander 100
Kilner, John 92
Kirk, John and Sons 116
knurr and spell 162
Koellanio, Signor 149
Lake Lock railroad 80
Lamb, William 101
Land, Eric 142
Lane, Richard 123
Lascelles, Henry 26, 36, 39
Lascelles, William S 37
Laurence, George 139
Lawe Hill 162-3
Lawrenson, Mrs 154
Leatham, W H 39
Lee, Henry 8, 58, 60
Lee, W H 140
Lee, George and Son 60, 84
Lee, Tottenham 84
Lever Bros 92
Lewis, Mrs 54
Liberal Association 39
Literary and Philosophical Society 122,
  143
Literary and Scientific Society 142
Lock-up 15, 23, 52
Lockwood and Mawson 86
Longley, Charles 134
Luddites 16-18
Lumb, Lucy 99, 101
Lupset Hall 43, 168, 169, 171
Lupton, Abraham 39, 162
Lynam, Mr 116
McDonnold, James 27-8, 68, 152
Mackie, Colonel 153
Mackie, Edith 163
Mackie, Robert B 40, 55, 119
Madden, W M
Maitland, Thomas 17
Malam, John 61
Malt 70
Manor of Wakefield 9, 33-36. 90
Market Cross 9, 91, 125
Markets 13, 28, 82, 86
  Borough 90, 124, 137, 153, 166
  Cattle 58, 89, 90 125
  Corn 69, 86-7

Marriott and Son 94
Marriott, Thomas 84
Marriott, W T 153
Marsland, Joseph 52, 82
Marsland, William 84
Masonic Lodges
  Sincerity 167
  Unanimity 88, 167
  Wakefield 167
Mechanics Institute 68, 80, 114
Mechanics Institution 94, 142-5, 157,
  160, 167
Metcalfe, Edward B 84
Mexborough, Earl of 88, 123
Micklethwaite, Daniel 82
Micklethwaite, Thomas 26, 65
Middleton, W C 153
Militia 15, 17
Mills
  Balne 84
  Bective 86
  Calder 86, 96
  Castle Bank 96
  Clarkson's 17
  Colbeck's 96
  Flanshaw 84, 101
  George Lee's 60, 85, 857
  Portobello 85-6, 96
  Rutland 86, 161
  Stonehouse's 85
  Westgate 85
Milner, Mary 133
Milnes, John 74, 158
Milnes, Pemberton 70
Milton, Viscount 36, 40
Mineral water 92
Mitchell, Edward 146
Model Lodging House 8
Moffatt, William L 87
Moore, Margaret 39
Moot Hall 25, 54
Morpeth, Lord 36, 39
Morris, George 111
Morton, Joseph 60
Mulligan, Norah 125
Muncaster, Jonathan 24
Mungo and shoddy 86
Music halls 64, 147, 152-3, 154
Music Saloon 19, 55, 101, 111-114,
  118, 135, 137, 143, 155-7, 159
Myers, J and B K 64
National Association of Sub
  Postmasters 64
Naylor, J and J 84
Naylor, Martin 64, 88, 115, 122, 143
Newnham, James 134
Newton, George 92
Newspapers 64-67
Nichols, James 146
Nichols, Thomas 65
Nicholson, William 94
Nostell Priory 153
Oakes, William 101-2
Oates, J E 50
Oliver, William 18
Orangery 133, 162
Overseers of the Poor 10, 14, 34, 46,
  48, 51, 52
Overthorpe Hall 119
Oxford Movement (Ritualism) 60, 106,
  108-9, 111-3, 116, 119
Panoramas 16 9
Parkin, George 34

Parkinson, Thomas 109
Paton, Noel 118
Paxton Society 34, 119, 162
Peache Trustees 113
Pemberton House 162
Pennefather, Somerset 111
Peterson, Andrew 109
Peterson, Mrs 45
Phillips, Perceval 147
Pickuls, S A 153
Pilkington, Lionel 57
Pilkington, Michael 126
Pilkington, Thomas 16
Pinfold 15
Pitman, Isaac 143
Plainsong Union 112
Poppleton, Richard 94
Porritt, W A 139
Post office 62-3, 87
Potts, William and Son 31
Pride, James Allan 111
Primrose League 40, 157
Probate Registry 10
Protestant Reformation Society 111
Public Rooms 29, 39, 43, 66, 143, 155,
  157, 170
Puckrin, William 111
Pye, William 117
Races 149, 170
Raikes, Robert 117, 126
Railway stations
  Kirkgate 64, 74, 114, 172
  Oakenshaw 74, 160
  Westgate 31, 64, 74-5
Ranger, William 28, 34, 56
Ranns, Joseph 64
Ratepayers' Association 27
Rayson, Benjamin 138
Reader, Dr 54
Rectory house 167
Red Hall, 56
Regattas 168-9
Registry of Deeds 9
Reservoirs 57, 59- 60
Rhodes, Joseph 9, 94, 139
Ripon Diocesan Board of Education 129
Ripon Diocesan Church Building
  Society 104
Rishworth House 41
Rishworth, Thomas 24, 41, 76, 111
Robinson, Disney 106, 110, 111, 113,
Robinson, Rebecca 110, 111, 114, 130
Robinson, G T 29
Robinson, John 65
Robinson, W L 147
Rogers, Thomas 26
Roller skating 170
RSPCA 166
Russell, Henry 157
Russell, Samuel 42
St John's Ambulance Association 45
St Joseph's Convent 135
St Oswald, Lord 153
Salkeld, Joseph 86
Salt, Titus 139
Salvation Army 103
Sandal Castle 165
Sanders, George 39
Sanderson, T K 40, 55, 153
Sankey, Ira David 115
Saunders, Master 149
Savile, Philip Yorke 124
Scarth, Margaret 135

Schools and colleges
  Alverthorpe 130, 133
  Apprentice 145
  Artisans' 133
  Bell (National) 127-9, 134-5
  Christ Church 130
  Cookery, 55
  Eastmoor 142
  Green Coat 122, 125-6, 134, 145
  Harrison's 138-9
  Holy Trinity 130, 137
  Industrial 138
  Infants 135
  Ings Rd 141
  Ladies Collegiate Academy 139
  Lancasterian 116, 127, 129, 135,
    137, 145
  Methodist 130
  Northern Congregational 126
  Private 138-9
  Proprietory 116, 123-4, 166
  Queen Elizabeth Grammar 117,
    119, 120, 122, 124-6
  Ragged 137
  St Andrew's 129-130
  St Austin's 134, 141
  St James's 130
  St John's 130, 141
  St Mary's 129
  St Michael's 130
  Sandal Endowed 122
  School of Art and Craft 145
  Silcoates 116, 121
  Smyth Street Academy 139
  Sunday 117, 126, 131, 137
  Thornes township 134
  Wakefield College 122, 145
  Wakefield Girls' High 119, 124-6
  Wakefield Technical and Art College
    119
  Westgate 141
  Writing 122
  Zion 131-3
Scoresby, Rev 143
Scott, Alexander 111
Scott, George Gilbert 108-9
Seal, Samuel 96, 100, 108
Seamless Steel Boat Co 94
Senior, Joseph 109
Senior, William 152
Seymour, Michael H 111
Sharp, John 104, 112, 139
Sharp, Mrs 45
Sharp, Samuel 8, 22, 61, 104, 155, 156,
  166, 170
Shaw, Benjamin 91
Shaw, E P 92
Shaw, Mr 21
Shaw, William 66, 101
Sherwood, Benjamin 153
Simpson, Edward 92
Simpson, Frederick 52
Simpson, Mrs 54
Sinclair, William 159
Smedley, Joseph 151
Smirthwaite, John G 167
Smith, George E 51
Smyth, J G 49, 162
Soke, The 8, 9, 29, 33-5, 57, 67, 92
Soulby, John 16
Spa 57
Stead, Robert 72
Steadman, Dr 102

Steers and Allott 67
Stonehouse, Matthew P 85
Storre, John 125
Stowell, Hugh 106
Strafford Gardens 161
Straton, Norman 119
Street Commissioners 9-11, 13-15, 22,
  26-8, 34, 60, 83
Strickland, George 39
Stubley, Ann 24
Stubley, George 24, 86
Stubley, James 86
Surveyors of Highways 10, 13, 28-9
Sutcliffe, Richard 92
Swallow, Joshua 24
Sweeting, J T 62
Sykes, Edward 29
Tait, William 112
Tammy Hall 31, 65, 85, 94
Tarbotton, Matthew Ogle 29, 57, 109
Tate, Thomas 146
Taylor, James 123, 137
Teall and Simpson 86
Teall, William 86
Tew, Percy 153
Thompson, Mrs 162
Thompson and Walker 68
Thorne, William S 153
Thornes House 36, 54
Thornton, Joseph 146
Thornton, W and D 93
Tootal, John 87
Tootal, John Battye 124, 160
Tootal, Thomas 24, 87
Tomlinson, W H B 111, 140
Tottenham, John 15-16
Town Hall 29-31, 60, 62, 94
Trustees of the Wakefield Poor see
  Governors of the Wakefield Charities
Tuke, William 47
Turnpike roads 73, 89
Tyas, George 69
Unity House 93
Vaux, John 91
Victoria, Queen 172
Volunteers 15, 16, 19, 52, 67, 152, 162, 168
Wade, Joseph 85-6
Wade, William Swift 52
Wainwright, Joseph 166
Wakefield Amateur Rowing Association 168
Wakefield Angling Club 168
Wakefield Bible Society 115
Wakefield Borough Cooperative Society
  92-3
Wakefield Borough Market Company
  28-9, 35, 62, 88, 90, 167
Wakefield Choral Society 165
Wakefield Conservative Association 67
Wakefield Corn Exchange Company
  13, 87
Wakefield Cycling Club 168
Wakefield and District Omnibus Co 73
Wakefield and District Organists'
  Association 166
Wakefield Farmers' Club 166
Wakefield Free Trade and Economic
  Flour Association 34
Wakefield Gaslight Company 61, 149
Wakefield Industrial Cooperative
  Society 92-3, 118
Wakefield Industrial and Fine Art
  Exhibition 94, 145
Wakefield Museum 122

Wakefield Naturalists' Society 168
Wakefield Rectory Manor 91
Wakefield School Board 8, 9, 62, 72,
  133, 138-9
Wakefield Society of Change-Ringers 126
Wakefield Swimming Club 170
Wakefield Temperance Society 67, 113-4
Wakefield Town Mission 100, 114
Wakefield Tradesmen's Association 76
Wakefield Trinity Football Club 157, 168
Wakefield Waterworks Co 57-60, 68
Wakefield Working Men's Conservative
  Association 40
Wakefield Working Men's Technical
  Association 68
Walker, Dr 57
Walker, J W 8, 24, 104
Walsh, James 141
Walton Hall 48, 92
Ward, Jonas 14
Ward, Thomas 84
Warren House 45
Waterton, Charles 111, 162
Watson and Pritchett 155
Watson, Charles 10
Watson, William 50, 52, 86, 94, 110, 141
Waxworks 159
Webber, William 155
Webster, James 141
Webster, Nathan 152
Weights and measures 23, 36
Wentworth, Godfrey 149
Wentworth House 125, 151
Westgate Common Cooperative Society 93
Westmorland, J J 91
West Riding Horticultural Society 166
Wharncliffe, Lord 36
Whiteley, John 66
Whitham, James 27, 29
Whitham, Samuel 85, 139-40
Whitworth, John 131
Wilberforce, William 26, 36
Wigglesworth, E 158
Wild, Mrs 153
Wild, T H 68
Wilderspin, Samuel 135
Wilkinson, John 149
Wilkinson, Tate 147
Willey, Jocelyn 106
Williams, George 114
Willis, Edward 158
Willis's Rooms 158-9
Winter, C 138
Womack, Samuel 72
Wombwell, George 159
Wombwell's menagerie 159
Wood, Robert 80
Wood, Thomas 18
Wood, William 11, 80, 155
Woolley Hall 149
Workhouse 48, 50, 52
Wortley, John Stuart 39
Wraith, James 146
Wroe, John 103
Yeomanry Cavalry 15-6, 18-19, 45,
  151, 157, 162
York, Duke of 165
Yorkshire Architectural Society 108
Yorkshire Council of Education 55
Young, John 84
Young, William 84
Young Men's Christian Association 114
Zetland, Earl of 167